YOU DO YOU

Edited by Jen Mann

SEVERAL SASSY SCRIBES

Throat Punch Media, LLC

OTHER BOOKS AVAILABLE

People I Want to Punch in the Throat: Competitive Crafters, Drop Off Despots, and Other Suburban Scourges

Spending the Holidays with People I Want to Punch in the Throat: Yuletide Yahoos, Ho-Ho-Humblebraggers, and Other Seasonal Scourges

Working with People I Want to Punch in the Throat: Cantankerous Clients, Micromanaging Minions, and Other Supercilious Scourges

My Lame Life: Queen of the Misfits

OTHER ANTHOLOGIES AVAILABLE

I Just Want to Pee Alone

I STILL Just Want to Pee Alone

I Just Want to Be Alone

I Just Want to Be Perfect

But Did You Die?

OTHER SINGLES AVAILABLE

Just a Few People I Want to Punch in the Throat (Vol. 1)
Just a Few People I Want to Punch in the Throat (Vol. 2)
Just a Few People I Want to Punch in the Throat (Vol. 3)
Just a Few People I Want to Punch in the Throat (Vol. 4)
Just a Few People I Want to Punch in the Throat (Vol. 5)
Just a Few People I Want to Punch in the Throat (Vol. 6)

CONTENTS

Here's to strong women.
May we know them.
May we be them.
May we raise them.

— UNKNOWN

INTRODUCTION

This book came about because a few years ago I was sitting in a parent teacher conference with my daughter's grade school teacher. His report was essentially: she's bright, but she goofs off and doesn't work up to her potential. I nodded automatically, because this was basically the same report I'd heard over the years. All of a sudden I realized he'd said something new. "Excuse me?" I asked.

"I was saying when we have group projects, she can be a bit bossy."

I stopped nodding. "What?"

"She takes over. She tends to order everyone around, rather than letting the group work as a whole, she takes on..."

"A leadership role?" I demanded.

He looked uncomfortable. (As he should.)

My son also takes charge of group projects and never once has a teacher called him bossy or packaged this trait as a negative. I sat there willing myself not to cry. Not because I was sad, but because I was furious. I am mad-crier. And when I mad-cry, men see that as a sign of weakness, when really they should be protecting their man bits with everything they have, because I'm looking for something to hit.

I was so angry that this man was an influential part of my daughter's life. He was going to be her teacher for the next year and he'd already made up his mind that she was bossy, and in his mind, that was a problem. He wasn't going to embrace her quirky nature and encourage her dark sense of humor. He wasn't going to nurture her abilities to be a natural leader, instead he was going tamp them down and remind her that girls are meant to be quiet and docile.

I took a deep breath and calmed my rage-shakes. "She's bossy, because she wants the project to be done the right way," I said. "You said she's bright and she's not working up to her potential and yet, when she tries to work up to her potential—to take charge and make sure a group project is getting done properly—you call her bossy. Got it. I think we're done here." I got up and left before I flipped a table.

Here's the thing, Mr. Teacher, I didn't raise my daughter to be a sheep. I didn't raise her to sit quietly on the sidelines and not advocate for herself. She'll be in middle school in a few years and we both know that middle school chews up little girls and spits them out. I am preparing her for war. I am building her self-confidence every day so that when life chips away at it she has reserves. If the worst thing you can say about her is she's bossy, then I see nothing wrong with her attitude.

You can call her "bossy," or "bitchy," or "shrill," or "opinionated," or whatever insult you want to hurl, but I will teach her that each one of those words aren't insults. They're powerful words when you own them. And she'll own every single one of them. She will also own "girly," and "beautiful," and "delicate," and when she wants to, "quiet." She will be her own person who will be confident in every situation she is thrown into, because she will know deep down in the core of her being who she is. She is all of these things, because she is a fierce and feisty girl who will grow up to be a fierce and feisty woman.

This book is for anyone who needs a little extra armor before a battle.

Jen Mann

TEN SIMPLE RULES FOR GIRLS TO FOLLOW

BY JULIE VICK

Being a girl is easy! You just have to follow a few simple rules:

10. Smiling: Don't smile too much – you'll send the wrong message. But do smile a little – not smiling makes you seem unapproachable and you want to be approached, just not by the wrong kind of people. Make sure your smile is genuine and not fake – somewhere between a creepy clown and a cheerleader.

9. Aggression: Don't be too aggressive – no one likes a pusher and once you start pushing it's probably only a matter of time before you are pushing meth. But stop being such a pushover. Any pushing you do should be moderate – like the amount of pressure you would apply to a vacuum.

8. Kids: Don't have kids, they will ruin your chance at a good career. Of course, if you don't have kids, you will be asked to justify the choice constantly, so it's best to have one kid. Except that one kid will grow up lonely without siblings, so have two; except two will make your life much more difficult and kill your chance at becoming the next Hillary Clinton. The perfect amount of kids is 1.75. Unfortunately, no one has yet figured out how to achieve it.

7. Clothing: Don't dress too revealing – you will invite unwanted attention. But don't be too frumpy – you don't want to avoid *all* attention. Aim for something between sexy and schoolmarm – like an extremely hip librarian.

6. Talking: Don't speak too loudly – you will come off as a bitch. Don't speak too softly – you will come off as too quiet. Speak at exactly 60 decibels so that people can hear you suggest valuable ideas in meetings, but someone can always talk over you.

5. Money: You will probably make less money than most men. But you should try to make more money than some men, just make sure one of them is not your husband.

4. Food: Don't eat too little – you need to get some meat on those bones! Don't eat too much – it's unladylike. Just constantly ask yourself one question: "Are you sure I should be eating that?"

3. Words: Stop adding qualifiers and words like "sorry" to your speech. Speak more like a man who barks orders at people, even if no one really likes being spoken to that way.

2. Brains: It's good to be smart – but not too smart. Only answer about one third of the questions you know correctly.

1. Rules: It's impossible to follow them all. So, it's best to start breaking them now.

JULIE VICK IS A WRITER AND MOM WHO LIVES IN COLORADO. HER work has appeared in New Yorker Daily Shouts, *Real Simple, Parents,* and *McSweeney's Internet Tendency. You can read more of her work at julievick.com and follow her on Twitter @vickjulie.*

❦ 2 ❦

GIRL STUFF

BY ABIGAIL CLARK

Inspired by Eve Ensler's "Embrace Your Inner Girl"

TO BE AN EMOTIONAL CREATURE IS TO FEEL EVERYTHING AS IF FOR the first time. To let it all overwhelm you with enthusiasm, accepting it as you would a gift. Or a handshake. Like looking at the floor of a glass-bottomed boat, seeing everything. Maybe not clearly, but at least seeing it all. You understand a little bit more, the uncertainty in the teenage boy's stance, why that little girl cried so hard when her sister flicked her nose. You sense the things that people rather wouldn't. On the Metro, that uncomfortable woman over there. She would rather not be talking to that man who speaks a lot and doesn't listen. Or the weariness that plagues the other woman's bones, how her colors seemed to fade just a little bit more.

You will be ostracized for caring when no one else does. The world will look at all your feeling and find something weak, worthless. Feminine.

I'm proud to be an emotional creature. I'm moved to tears often— in government class, at a concert, when my mom wakes me up too

3

early. I like it. It's like my superpower, seeming to make everything that much brighter. I like the way the world seems to course through my veins, offer up these little gifts, allow me to feel something so sure that something gets left behind.

People would rather not be that way. Many of my teachers have lectured on the value of restraint, moderation, toning it down. I don't see the point. Why make yourself smaller? Why allow yourself to shrink for the sake of other people's comfort? Why give away your ability to live with unadulterated feeling?

Is there no power in deciding with your heart? Your conscience? Is there no logic in seeing and feeling the situation of another, and taking that into consideration? And isn't intuition knowing, in one way or another?

I don't know. I'm just 16. I think I like being 16. I liked being 13. Fourteen was bearable. Fifteen better. But *16*... what an age! There's a kind of roundness to it. Eight times two is 16, eight divided by two is four, four times four is 16. There's a brightness to it, deeming it important in some way.

But 16 also feels like an in-between place. A little bit lonely, a little bit not. Sixteen feels like a precipice over something that could be wonderful.

I wish I had relished being a little girl more. Being 16 is fun; being a little girl more so. You're able to see things that aren't really there – things that make reality a little more fantastic, a little more bewitching. When I was around four, I decided to only wear dresses. I felt beautiful every day. The world belonged to me. It consisted of my mom, my dad, my two brothers, and my best friend that lived next door. It consisted of my dog, still skinny then, the solidness of my grandmother's bones, smelling faintly of detergent and cigarettes. It was the afternoon sun filtering through leaves. Everything feels bigger when you're four. Everything feels more, and there's a little bit of magic in all that feeling.

When does that leave us? When do we decide to give away our intensity? When do we become indifferent?

Maybe when people decide we should. Our capacity for compassion is a muscle we stop working once it becomes hard to do so. When it starts to become inconvenient, as we grow bigger, different values are infused into us: logic, power, strength. Compassion is illogical. Empathy is weakness. Be reasonable. Man up.

One time my mom was worried about one of her students, and wanted to check on her. We drove to their temporary house, and it was apparent that she and her family had been evicted. All I can remember is the sight of her toys lined up by the mailbox as it rained, as if they were waiting. All I could imagine was the little girl who had to leave all of her toys behind. Who cared that she was gone, other than her family and her school teacher?

I've recently read about shootings in the United States. I don't think I cried when I read the names of the people that were killed. I have to wonder, who did? Is there anyone left who hasn't been desensitized? Who thinks about the shootings that don't make news headlines? Who really feels the horror of those deaths, other than the lives they directly affect?

I don't think about it as much as I used to.

I worry about little girls a lot. I worry about how I ended up where I am, about what happened to the little girl I used to be. I never used to temper myself. I felt no shame. Now I worry about my friends. I ask them to text me when they get home, just in case something happens. I teach the younger girls to hold their phone to their ear when they feel unsafe walking alone. My driving education teacher told the girls in our class that if we were ever being followed by a police cruiser, we should call the police, just to make sure it's not someone else entirely, someone who wants to hurt you. You learn to hold your keys between your fingers. You learn to tell yourself that it doesn't really matter; your fear isn't real. It doesn't matter. You're overreacting. Don't trust that feeling. Ignore your intuition. Stop exaggerating. We're girls. It's what we do.

Women have this magic drained out of them through the years. Their compassion, their wonder, their girl stuff becomes a pale, shriveled thing. It slows you down. Why keep it?

But that's the thing. Keeping it locked away is how we got to now. It's how boys are bled of their humanity and girls are punished because of it. It's how we have allowed ourselves to forget the suffering of the

5

world and take it as a given. It's how we justify our failings and blame others.

But imagine with me for a moment. What would happen if we used that magic instead of keeping it hidden? What would happen if we prided ourselves on our ability to empathize, to feel unapologetically? If in doing that, what if we created a culture of empathy that everyone could be part of?

What would happen if our politicians accepted a culture of empathy? Would there still be massacres? Would politics and policy change? Would there still be laws incarcerating groups by the thousands? Would people use GoFundMe.com to pay for their cancer treatment? Would there still be as few women and minorities in government as there are now? Would people be paid a livable wage? Would there still be casual racism and sexism at work? Would people lobby for justice and compassion?

What would happen if *we all* embraced our girl stuff? Would we read the news more? Would it affect us? Would we argue as much as we do? Would we understand each other more? Would we try to change the things we cannot accept?

I like to imagine this world sometimes. I like to picture what would happen if we stopped killing the girl stuff in us: the stuff that still cries at suffering. The stuff that looks at the wonder of the world with wide eyes and an open heart.

When we embrace our girl stuff, we become so much more. We become vibrant, beautiful creatures to behold. We're all so different. We're all intelligent, passionate, soft, strong, hilarious, hardened, bold, independent, young, old, brighter than colors themselves. The world needs us. The world needs that part of us. When we stop being ashamed of it, the girl stuff, that's when things start to happen.

I have a friend who cussed out the boys that said gross things to the girls in gym class. I have a friend who speaks with a soft, lilting tone, like a kind of music, when she talks about her art. I have a friend who wears huge hoop earrings and has a grin in her voice. I have a friend that wants to do good things, and works hard at her abilities to spread goodness. They laugh like girls, guarded yet open, shy yet unflinching, delighting in it all.

I like to think we're all connected by a single thin thread, constantly pulling and releasing pressure. Maybe the whole world is connected by these threads, linking our minds and hearts, but only for moments. Seconds. We forget about the threads, but briefly, we remember. And we're overcome by it all, how clear and complicated it can all be, all the hurt and love there can be. Call it a new String Theory.

ABIGAIL CLARK IS 16 YEARS OLD AND HAS WRITTEN MANY WORDS. At least 12. She aspires to write many more. She hails from northern Virginia, where she likes to dance, especially contemporary and modern. She also plays the string bass (the big, wood one). She's a well-rounded gal. When she's not engaging in these various activities, she exists in a vague state of outrage, as a result of womanhood. This is her first publication.

❦ 3 ❧

BE YOUR OWN DAMN ROCK

BY JULIA ARNOLD

Despite women all over the media demanding equal rights and equal pay for the last year, it was also a year of women declaring all over social media how grateful they were for the "rock" in their lives. At least it felt that way to me. While on the surface, I suppose, it's a nice compliment: telling someone you are grateful for their support. But scratch—or merely dust—the surface of that statement, and I had to suppress extreme, indulgent eye rolls every time I read it. I was increasingly confused and annoyed every time I read it.

I swear after I read about one woman's beloved rock, I couldn't turn on my phone without another rock being hailed on Facebook or Instagram. In one sitting, I kid you not, I read an adult daughter profusely thanking her father for being her rock, and then I saw another one where a woman declared her husband to be her rock on his birthday. I'm sure there were plenty of other examples across the web that I never even saw. *Why were so many women giving so much credit to so many men?* I was ready to throw up and throw out my computer.

Why did it bother me so much? I asked myself that same question, and it didn't take me long to flesh it out.

I looked over at my own daughter, age five and totally fearless, wearing one of her self-styled outfits where every color in the rainbow and every pattern possible must be visible. She is blissfully unaware of truly difficult struggles; her biggest concerns are usually along the lines of a scratch on her knee, bickering with her big brother, or how mean her mom is for saying it's time to leave the park and head home. She's tough and funny and full of life and, frankly, everything you'd want in a child. I have no fear about the woman she will become and the wonderful things she will accomplish—all on her own.

All these rock statements also made me think about my own life. I realized I've never had anyone I would call my rock – and that's not a sad, selfish, or negative thing. I appreciate anyone who gives me encouragement and support, but I own my hard work and any success I've had. I think that's a good thing, and it's something I want my children to feel as well. I am my own rock, and I want my daughter to be her own damn rock, too.

Part of what especially bugs me when women attribute someone to be their "rock" is that someone is usually male. How can we call ourselves independent, strong women and demand to be treated equally to men, and then in the very same breath, give someone else— a man—the credit for our getting us to, or keeping us in, a good place in our lives? Because that's what it sounds like. It sounds something like: "I've been through a lot in life and couldn't have done it—any of it —without my ROCK." *Is it bugging you yet?*

I don't remember a rock—male or female—surviving the brutal middle or high school years for me, or attending my college classes for me (especially the 8 a.m. Friday ones). I don't remember some personified rock getting my first (or subsequent jobs) for me. I did the interview. I had the experience. There was no one holding my hand in the interviews or drafting my resume a million times. And I sure as hell don't remember any rock carrying my babies for me for over the course of nine months and then enduring having them surgically removed. I'm exhausted just thinking about all of it.

Life is full of challenges, and the old adage is true: what doesn't kill us makes us stronger. Each one of us who gets up every morning and hauls ass is living proof of it. We live by the choices we make and we deserve to own our successes and triumphs.

No one does these tough, challenging things for us, especially some rock we're giving the credit to. Let's take ownership of our struggles and our accomplishments and be proud of them. *That's* what I want my daughter to be spouting off online if social media is still such a constant in 10 years (and I pray it isn't). I never want to hear her say "Thank you for being my rock" unless she's thanking herself.

The good news is that I think I might be on the right track. A few months ago, my five-year-old daughter was shooting rubber bands with a young boy on the floor of a waiting room while my son was in a piano lesson. I warned my spunky little girl not to let a rubber band fly into her new friend's face. The boy's father immediately stepped in and said, "Oh don't worry, he's tough. He's a boy." My daughter stopped what she was doing, furrowed her brow and thought deeply. I opened my mouth to stick up for her and girls everywhere. But before the words came out, my kid looked up at the man and clearly and confidently explained the facts: "I can be tough, too, you know." I closed my mouth and smiled, feeling beyond proud. I was not her rock. She was her own rock.

At the end of the day, I feel at my core that we should be able to make it through the hard times ourselves. We don't need someone to do it for us. Yes, we all need steady support and a nice, hard hug now and then, but we can be our own rocks. Our daughters are listening to us *all the time*. Let's let them hear how their mothers stand on their own remarkable feet.

JULIA ARNOLD IS A WRITER LIVING IN MINNESOTA WITH HER husband, two children, and rapidly growing collection of animals. She writes about parenting, equestrian pursuits, animal welfare, and more. Her work has appeared in publications such as Horse Illustrated, Young Rider, Dressage Today, The Morgan Horse, Mother.ly, *and* Mamalode. *She blogs with humor and honesty at FranticMama.com. Her author site is JuliaStarrArnold.com. Julia has loved writing for as long as she can remember and thinks it is entirely possible she was born with a pencil in her hand.*

❧ 4 ❧

VOICE

BY MADDIE BELDEN

I may not be strong
I may not be tall
And I may not be loud
But I have an opinion
And I have a right
A right to be heard
A right to stand for myself
So we all must stand for ourselves
If we hope to make a difference
In this world of darkness
We can be the light
Because our differences
Give us a voice
A voice that is our own
A voice that shines a light
A light in the darkness
And sometimes we just need the light
To guide us on our way

MADDIE BELDEN is a middle schooler with a love of books, mismatched socks, and her crazy cocker spaniel, Macy. She has written many poems and short stories, but this is her first published piece. When she isn't reading or writing, she can be found sewing, daydreaming at her desk, or plotting to take over the world.

UNAPOLOGETICALLY ME

BY SHYA GIBBONS

I have spent the past 30 years of my life apologizing. I apologized profusely for things I didn't even have to apologize for. I was not the child who rebelled and had to constantly see the principal or be put in time out; I was the opposite. I didn't even toe the line. I set up camp far past the line on the safe side, which led me to become overly polite and apologize profusely for everything. Every single thing. I apologized when I did nothing wrong. I apologized for being my strange, quirky self. I spent so long apologizing and thinking I was to blame for everything that at some point along the years I forgot I was my own person with my own feelings. I was not responsible for every other soul on this earth.

Let me back up some. Way back to kindergarten which seems like yesterday, but it was really 25 years ago. Our teacher gave us a simple writing prompt: A horse escapes into the woods, what happens next? The other children said that the farmer went looking for the horse. Some said the horse made its way back to the farm on its own eventually. Not me. No, I wrote that the woods were actually magical and once the horse broke free it turned into what it had always felt like it was destined to be – a unicorn. As soon as it escaped its pen, the horse, now turned unicorn, was free to be the magical, amazing beast it was always meant to be. My teacher told my mother I was adamant the scenario could happen. This story has always been one of my mother's favorite stories to tell people when I talk about how much writing means to me.

Alas, my brush with pushing authority by arguing about turning horses into unicorns started and ended with that assignment. From then on, I was the odd girl who kept to herself, which I was and totally own up to. I marched to the beat to my own drum. I desperately wanted to find my way into a clique; I spent countless hours crying because I could never quite find my group of kindred spirits. I wasn't pretty enough to be popular, I wasn't athletic enough to participate in sports. I was the girl who doodled the name of my crush all over my books. I was the girl who had so many pictures of her favorite celebrity taped up in her locker that it was essentially a shrine. I wrote during free periods at school, went home to complete my homework, and spend the rest of the time writing.

While computers and televisions weren't common for teenagers that age to have in their room (yikes, I am old!) my parents trusted me enough to have both, as long as my grades didn't suffer. I'm eternally grateful they did because I lived and breathed through Word documents. As the weird girl I definitely caught some heat at school for it and on days where it overwhelmed me and consumed my every thought, I would simply leave this world and write a new one.

It was through writing that I made a stunning surprise: I had the ability to become my own heroine.

I became the lead of any story that I wanted or needed at that time. If I needed something serious, I would write a serious book. If I needed emotional support, I would write a story where a man professed his love over and over again. I went from feeling like a puppet with everyone pulling the strings to the master. The page was the one place I let myself be truly myself.

If I wasn't writing then I was daydreaming. I always wanted to have a career where I made a difference in people's lives. There is the saying that you can't save everyone, but I didn't care. I was going to try my hardest to help every person I could. And I like to think I did to the best of my ability.

I helped people through abusive relationships, problems in college, problems at work. I loved it. It became emotionally draining eventually, but I knew by depleting the levels in my tank I was replenishing someone else's. People came and went in my life, usually after I was used as their emotional dumpster and they moved on. Where it would make other people angry, I didn't care. My thought was God gave me the chance to change someone's life for a moment and that's all I saw it as. I was happy to be given opportunities to see a side of people not many were privileged enough to have seen. I loved seeing them move past their hurdles and continue on to flourish. But eventually a car running on fumes quits; it gives its absolute best until it physically can't any more. My fumes ran out recently, which led me to realize a lot of things about myself, both good and bad.

Having had bouts and depression and anxiety off and on from a young age I was guilty of sometimes shutting myself off from friends. I would go radio silence and throw myself into writing. The same escape as always, the same soothing and safe place I have had for decades.

My 11-year-old niece has recently started writing and I keep encouraging her and offering ideas for her to expand upon. I remind her she is amazing and has endless potential with her future. I tell her about things that happened to me at school and how I used writing as an outlet. I told her that if she keeps searching she can find something that makes her heart soar the way mine does with writing, even if her heart is stuck at the bottom of a canyon. She is our future and I keep encouraging her with whatever project she is working on, whether it is writing or designing clothes.

While I have other negative things that I realized about myself lately, I forced myself into a very difficult challenge: find good in yourself. I'm a firm believer that people are intrinsically good and I give people the benefit of the doubt more often than I should. The only person I never afforded that same luxury to was myself. No one could be harder on me or knock me down lower than I did. I have been mentally beating myself up for as long as I can remember. Nothing was ever good enough in my eyes and I always told myself that.

It's hard to break that habit. A habit of 20-some years of overly harsh, critical thinking is hard to stop. It was amusing in a sardonic way that the girl who could find good in everyone else couldn't find any redeemable attributes in herself. I'm still struggling with it, to be honest.

Not too long ago I realized that I apologize for everything, including things I do that are harmless and are simply part of who I am. I would apologize for being emotional and crying when I was happy, or cry when I was sad. I cry constantly. I'm an empath and I'm done apologizing for crying when I'm overwhelmed with emotion. Some people pride themselves on the fact that they can't remember the last time they cried, and while I think that's fine, I know that will never be who I am. It finally sunk in when I was shopping at a big-name store. I had my cart tucked against the shelves, out of the way while I looked at a selection of toys. A woman comes down the aisle and slams into my cart, which there was no need for because I had made sure when I positioned my cart that it wouldn't clog up the aisles for other shoppers. I instantly felt horrible and started to apologize. She ignored me and continued on her way without a single word spoken back to me. My first thought was: How rude the woman was for not extending any words back like, "These things happen" or "No big deal." My second thought was: Wait a minute. She hit me. She didn't say "excuse me" to indicate she needed to pass on the slim chance I was blocking her path. Nothing. What exactly had I been profusely apologizing for? Getting hit? Being ignored as I tried to exchange pleasantries? I had not one, single reason for why I felt that situation deemed an apology from me.

I realized that I apologized about a lot, but more than anything I apologized for who I was. When someone points out that I have a fictional character on the screen of my phone I say, "I know. It's weird. I'm sorry." When my OCD is really bad and someone sees me washing my hands three times in a row I repeat the same as above: "I know. It's weird. I'm sorry."

No.

Nope.

Not anymore. I am done apologizing about everything. I do not need to defend my quirks to anyone. They are what makes me me, after all. It has been a long journey to finally reach this peak where I don't care what others think about me or the things they deem "weird" or "odd." Every person has one thing they do that others would find strange and I think it's time to stop judging people for their choices. Unlocking my phone and seeing that character makes me happy, and I will never again apologize for something that makes me smile when the world is full of frowns.

My best advice to every person, no matter the age, is: You do you. You do what makes you happy. Do what soothes your soul (within reason, of course!). Don't worry about what others might say or think. Worry about yourself and your own happiness. Keep a fire burning inside of you for something whether it is writing, knitting, chopping wood, or playing video games. Every person needs one thing that makes them come alive, and I know that I am incredibly lucky to have figured out at a young age that that thing for me is writing.

Go show the world who you are—the REAL you. Don't put limitations on yourself for fear of being ridiculed or judged. Chances are if people make fun of you for something that makes you happy, they probably aren't the kind of people you want to be friends with anyway. From here on out I plan to be unapologetically me. I hope you find the power inside yourself to be the same way. It is quite freeing.

SHYA GIBBONS IS THE FOUNDER OF THE FACEBOOK COMMUNITY Vintage Dreams With A Modern Twist and a contributor to I Just Want To Be Perfect. *Her work has appeared on* Sammiches & Psych Meds *and* McSweeney's. *She is happily married to an incredible man who doubles as her best friend. They have a five-year-old boy who lights up their life. Check out her work on Facebook and tell her "Hi" when you stop by, she loves meeting new people.*

WISHES FOR A TWEEN GIRL

BY GALIT BREEN

My girls' birthdays are only four days (and two years) apart. For the past few years, we've celebrated on or around their March birth dates. But this year, our family traded in our usual one-weekend-after-another separate celebrations for a last-day-of-school, hot summer night, everyone-piled-into-the-yard-and-by-the-fire-pit-and-into-our-basement kind of celebration. And it was glorious.

I watched and listened to and heard an absolute gaggle of girls—some of whom I've known since their chubby fingers wrapped around thick crayons as they learned to write their names and thank-you notes and stories, tongues sticking through pursed lips, brows furrowed, smile and eyes lit at success. And others I'm just getting to know, learning what that laugh or this look means. And in that watching and listening and hearing, I was overwhelmed. With their noise and their movement and their talking, yes. But also by their goodness.

And if it wouldn't have been a horrid interruption of their night, here's what I would've said to them by the light of the fire or the stars or the movie.

To the ones with the loudest laugh, the first joke, the cleverest of responses—keep using your voice and your humor. A laugh that can be picked out in a crowd is a gift.

To the athletes, the enviable ball spikers and the perfect hand-spring executors and the swift runners, keep at it. Strength comes in many forms, and this is one of them. Own it.

To the joiners, you're absolutely right—why *not* you? Confidence makes the world go 'round, and you've got it. Hold on tight. It belongs to you.

To the storytellers, keep talking and telling and weaving. It's your story, so tell it. You're the only one who can.

To the quiet ones in the back, I see you. You are understated, and you are important. These things can, and do, go hand in hand.

To the whip-smart ones with all of the answers, you keep flexing those muscles. A smart woman can make the world go round.

To the caretakers, you have it just right. We are meant to take care of each other.

To the ones with the dirty feet and the abandoned shoes, who needs shoes anyway? Don't be afraid to get dirty, to be you, to get the most out of every moment. It's true what your mom and I say – it does all go by so fast. Grasp the moment, the dandelion, the grass, and skip the shoes.

To the leaders, the ones who ran the show and organized the games and kept everyone moving along: That's called leadership, and it's a coveted skill. Anyone who calls it anything different (and negative) is wrong.

To the ones who led by example, followed the unwritten rules, made sure that everyone got their fair share, this, too, is leadership. It's quiet, but powerful and just as coveted.

In so much of life, women demand *different* and *change* of ourselves and of each other. *Not enoughs* and *shoulds* and *shouldn'ts* slip between our lips all too easily and quickly. *Not pretty enough, not smart enough, not popular enough. Too pretty, too smart, too popular.*

But what I learned from watching a group of just-out-of-school tweens on a hot summer night is that right here and right now, they have the exact right idea. So the thread in my wishes for tween girls—

the understated ones and the caretakers and the athletes and the joke-sters—is this:

Trust yourselves and your instincts and your goodness.

Allow input from the world to do nothing but build on what is already pretty amazing – you.

And see how each of your shines doesn't dim the others.

My wish for you is to keep being exactly who you are.

GALIT BREEN IS THE BESTSELLING AUTHOR OF KINDNESS WINS, A guide to teaching your child to be kind online; the TEDx Talk, "Raising a Digital Kid Without Having Been One;" and the Facebook group The Savvy Parents Club. Her writing has been featured on The Huffington Post, The Washington Post, Buzzfeed, TIME, *and more. She lives in Minnesota with her husband, three children, and ridiculously spoiled mini goldendoodle. Find her at TheseLittleWaves.net.*

JUST CALL HER MADAME

BY MAI WEN

"Life's not fair."

This was what I was told. No, I wasn't whining about my friend's newer and bigger house, or the neighbor's brand new car. I was asking why there was only a mother-son dodgeball tournament at my nine-year-old daughter's school, and none for girls. There was a father-daughter dance, was the first counter. But my daughter went to that the year before and found it "so soooo *boring*, Mom. I want to play dodgeball. Why can't I?"

They question hung on me like a wet towel. I felt ashamed that I hadn't really questioned the sexism of these Parent Teacher Organization (PTO) sponsored events before she pointed it out. I knew that it was sexist, but it was an accepted form of sexism that I didn't always bother to see. But once she put the question on me, I couldn't shake it off. I'm a feminist, after all – a strong female who has survived a lot and fought for what I wanted out of life. Growing up with a Chinese, strongly patriarchal family I remember early on resenting the suggestion that in any way I was inferior to boys. When I'd go out to help carry in the groceries and my aunts would chide me, telling me it was men's work, I'd double my load. It's a stubbornness that is only triggered in me when I'm told what I can't do, and in many ways, it has served me well. Perhaps it was the hypocrisy of my family's patriarchal beliefs that gave me the courage to fight against it. They told me that men were the heads of the household, and yet it was my mother and aunts who worked as computer programmers and supported their families. My mother was a single mom, my aunt was as well briefly before she remarried, and my other aunt took care of my uncle and grandma. They showed me a very different version of women than what they told me. As with most children, I believed what I saw more than what I was told.

And so, I was triggered. That *can't* word ringing in my ears and firming my resolve. I turned my daughter's question "Why can't I?" into what I thought was an innocent email to the PTO president.

Years before, our family had moved to Franklin, Tennessee, from Raleigh, North Carolina. Although both are considered the South, Research Triangle Park and the multiple colleges in Raleigh made it a hub for transplants and diversity. Moving to Franklin, I was worried about the lack of diversity, but immediately found the people the friendliest I'd ever met. My hopes rose and then promptly fell when my daughter started kindergarten. The first offense: after school club forms came home. My daughter, ever the creative mind and active hands, loved Legos. I found the Lego club listed and directly under the title were the horrifying words: *boys only*. Something like bile rose in my throat, but it was far worse than bile. It was a mixture of shock, disbelief, and absolute terror. Being raised in liberal Minnesota, this sort of thing never happened growing up. Boys were required to take Home Economics just as girls were required to take shop class. The fear of raising my children in this culture sent me reeling and I fought the people-pleaser inside of me and emailed the organizers, politely asking why the Lego club was "boys only." The response was even worse than I expected: The sons of the moms who volunteered to run the club wanted the club to be boys only, so to please their sons, the moms requested to exclude girls.

Insert open-mouthed emoji here.

Not only are they excluding girls at a school PTO-sponsored activity, but they are also teaching boys as young as five that their every whim will be honored, even if it excludes a whole group of people.

Needless to say, my mama-bear claws came out and I may have thrown an analogy at the PTO saying that since I'm Asian, would it be okay if I started an after school club and only allowed Asians to be a part of it? I never received a response to my last email, but they never had "boys only" or "girls only" clubs again. Mommy win even if the PTO hated me.

Fast forward to the dodgeball email. I received a couple of truncated and unsatisfactory responses telling me they'd discuss it and then suggesting that my daughter join a dodgeball after school club. The PTO President even advertised that there were no gender limitations on the clubs, obviously unaware that it was thanks to me. My daughter couldn't do the club because of other obligations, I told her, and asked her to keep me informed on their discussions.

Meanwhile, my daughter, tall and lanky like her father – dark, silky hair always pulled back in a low ponytail, came home from school every day and asked me if I'd heard about dodgeball yet. After a week of no updates, mama-bear claws started to itch at my fingertips again. I acquiesced and emailed. I listed all the people being excluded from the event the way it currently was set up: mothers without sons, sons without mothers, same-sex couples will either have no moms to go, or will have to pick which mom, and, of course, girls. I suggested some possible solutions. Could we have two different nights of dodgeball and scrap the kind of creepy father-daughter dance? Could we say parent-child dodgeball tournament? I even offered to be in charge of planning it next year. I thought it was a pretty convincing email.

Boom.

I got no response. I started to get frustrated. Finally, I hear from a friend that my email has been sent up to the principal to send to legal and is now an officially documented complaint. And the whole PTO board hates me. Again.

I don't like being hated. It causes my anxiety to go through the roof. I wish I didn't care, but I do. But even more, I don't like my daughter being told at the age of nine that you can't do something purely because you're a girl.

This is where I'm told to tell my daughter life's not fair. Twice by two different people.

The first was my friend who is on the PTO board and who told me about the ruckus my email caused. She told me that her daughter would rather play dodgeball than go to the father-daughter dance as well, but that she just told her daughter "life's not fair."

Next, the PTO President called me. She's a very sweet person and we talked out how everything went down. I didn't mean for things to get all "legal" and she admitted she should have just called me to talk things out with me from the beginning rather than putting me off. It was a good conversation until she told me about how her two boys always want the same video games that their friends have and she tells them, "life's not fair." She compared my daughter not getting to do an activity because she's a girl to her sons not getting spoiled by getting whatever video game they want. And what is my friend's message to her daughter? That "life's not fair" because girls don't get to do all the things boys can, and instead of fighting and pushing against it you just need to shut up and accept it?

Everything in me reels against these messages. I refuse to teach my daughter to shut up and accept sexism, even if that means I must be hated. It's a small price to pay to empower my daughter. My daughter who can run and play sports with the boys and then the next day play animals with the girls; who doesn't feel the need to play to any gender stereotype and instead rests in her own unique spot in the middle. My daughter who loves Harry Potter and Star Wars. Once while playing a game of Family Feud and the question was, "What should grooms be taught to say to their future wives?" instead of the popular responses of "You're right" and "Yes," she wrote down "Madame." When we were confused by this answer, she affected a haughty butler face and stiffly waved her hand in front of her and said in a very British accent, "*Ma*-dom." Apparently that's how my daughter expects to be addressed by her future spouse if she so chooses to get married.

I can't change the whole world and there are some like-minded friends who live in Franklin who talk about moving away because they can't stand the conservative, old-fashioned views here. But I actually love Franklin. I love the small-town feel and the friendly people (even if we vastly differ in life views). I love all the kid-friendly activities and weather. And what happens if I do move my family away to someplace more liberal? What opportunities would I have to teach my daughter to fight against sexism and other bigotry? What positive changes can I make in communities that already adhere to my beliefs? Here, as frustrating, difficult and sometimes horrifying it is, I can make a difference. I can teach my children that just because something is a certain way, it doesn't mean it's right. And better yet, that *they* can do something to affect change.

So call her Madame. Let her play dodgeball. Let her build Legos. Many argue that no one is stopping her. She can, and does, do these things at home. But it's the message that could stop her if we let it. The message that while you can do these things in the privacy of your home, there's no place for girls doing these things in the world.

And as we all know, kids learn more by what we do than what we say.

MAI WEN IS A FORMER SOCIAL WORKER AND CURRENT CHAUFFEUR TO three lovely children. She is also an aspiring novelist with two completed young adult science fiction manuscripts and working on an adult fantasy. Her novels contain strong social, women's and mental health issues but with a dose of time travel or magic (pick your poison, she's got both). If interested in learning more about her work you can find her on social media at @maiwenwriter.

LOOKING FOR LAUGHS IN ALL
THE WRONG PLACES

BY SHERRY STANFA-STANLEY

Slumped over a table in the basement of St. Patrick's of Heatherdowns Grade School, I grew bored with yet another evening of my Brownie troop's lame crafts.

As our leader demonstrated how to make tacky holiday wreaths— by tying colored tissue paper around wire clothes hangers bent into circles—I nudged the second-grade girls on either side of me.

"Who would hang that on their door? It looks like something that belongs wrapped around a toilet seat," I faux-whispered, "where everyone can crap on it."

My Brownie buddies roared.

Spurred on by their laughter, I managed to spout out another joke. And then another. By the end of the evening, potty humor proved to be a far bigger hit than lavatory decorations among the age seven crowd.

I leaned back and glanced around the table. I knew right then that, for me, making people laugh was far more rewarding than any condoned activity. I grinned in self-satisfaction.

By the fifth grade, I had already acquired the reputation of class clown. It also was right about this time that the head leader of my Scout troop, who *oddly* did not appreciate my humor, decided I was an unwelcome distraction. Not only did I not fly up to Cadets, I was booted from the troop.

Regardless, I could get used to entertaining an audience, even if I was looking for laughs in all the wrong places.

I continued to entertain my classmates in other unsanctioned and irreverent ways, like initiating games of truth or dare during our Catholic grade school masses and later using the Resusci Annie dummy as a dance partner—rather than an intended CPR tool—during high school health class.

Along the way, I also found another, more authority-acceptable venue for my humor. I began honing my writing skills.

I wrote poetry and short stories, specializing even then in humor and satire. On one of my sixth-grade papers, my teacher wrote, "If you don't do something with all of your talent, I'm going to come back and haunt you some day." (Side note: She didn't need to haunt me. We have become Facebook friends, and I acknowledged her early encouragement in my first book.)

Being named editor of my high school newspaper cemented the idea of a writing career. But what proved just as rewarding that same year was having my senior class vote me as "Best Sense of Humor." That accolade—sadly—didn't win me a single college scholarship, yet it did reaffirm that I was funny.

Sure, I could make people laugh. I had that going for me. But what I didn't gain until much, *much* later was the ability to laugh at myself.

A few years after my Brownies experience, I sat cross-legged on that same basement floor with my seventh-grade class, watching a holiday school program. Whether it was due to something I ate for lunch, or else just ill-fated timing, my gastric system chose that moment to make its distressed voice heard.

It's often difficult within a crowd to pinpoint the culprit of even the *loudest* intestinal explosion. I can only assume my mortified expression gave me away. When my "friends" seated closest to me promptly figured it out, they showed me no mercy. They elbowed me and simultaneously shouted, "Sherry!" This was followed by multiple animated exclamations of how gross and disgusting I was.

Everyone in the room, including the popular blond-haired boy I was secretly crushing on, turned and laughed at me. I did not laugh. In fact, if it hadn't required scrambling over a hundred classmates, I would have crawled right into a corner and died.

It wasn't until I tossed in bed that night, still horrified by my public farting fiasco, that I realized I should have reacted that afternoon by making a joke. It was a missed opportunity to salvage my self-esteem and win over the crowd with humor, instead of feeling defeated by the all-too-common awfulness of adolescent embarrassment.

But self-deprecating humor is lost on the average 12-year-old. In truth, most of us *never* really learn to laugh at ourselves.

I continued, as all of us do, to humiliate myself on countless occasions through adolescence and adulthood.

While rappelling down a cliff during a high school trip, I discovered the safety harness had somehow become entangled in my shirt. My shirt was already hiked above my belly button.

I contemplated this lose-lose situation: I could attempt to unhook the harness and crash to my death, or I could continue descending and allow the cable and my shirt to keep rolling up toward my shoulders. I finally choose the latter, providing the group below with an unplanned peep show. Not only was I mortified, but the crowd appeared less than impressed with what they viewed.

I avoided eye contact, during the remainder of the trip, with everyone.

Years later, as a young adult, I worked up the courage to try out for a community play. I hoped the entertainer within me might lead to a powerful stage presence. But when the director unexpectedly asked me to sing and dance, my mouth dropped—along with all my self-confidence. I'd never even sung in a school choir, and my old friend Resusci Annie was probably a better dancer than I was.

I had no other option, other than refusing and running from the room, which didn't seem likely to save my pride either. So, I bellowed a Christmas carol and danced—or rather *tripped*—across the stage. Looking out, I observed the director and her colleague nudge each other and grin. It was my first—and my very last—audition.

And, I experienced perhaps the most mortifying moment of all as a presumably grown-up and established business professional. While intending to email a few friends, I inadvertently sent an off-color joke to my company's *entire board of trustees.*

As I realized my mistake, I stared at my computer screen, paralyzed. And then my head dropped. "Good Lord," I prayed, with my hands covering my bowed head, "please let them all have good humor."

Although some mortification hits harder than others, none of us is immune to just-kill-me moments. We all make mistakes and endure personal mishaps. We all find ourselves cringing and cowering in embarrassing situations. We all prove to be—and far too often while in *public*—imperfect.

Yet it's how we react to our displays of humiliating inadequacies or blunders that makes the difference.

A few years ago, I concluded I was tired of living with a suffocating sense of self-consciousness and fear of judgment. I'd grown tired of desperately trying to live my life in the safe zone.

So, I embarked on a year of weekly experiences that each fell far outside my comfort zone. While I hoped these 52 ventures might enlighten me in some way, I knew they also would test me, frighten me, and humiliate me. Holy Hell! What was I thinking?

I went through with them anyway.

I performed in public as a mime, even though my own lack of fondness for mimes was mirrored that day by many passersby. If mimes weren't sworn to silence, I would have screamed "Wait, come back!" to all those who rolled their eyes and scurried away.

I bared it all at a nude beach, with my (clothed) 75-year-old mother in tow. Even *she* refused to sit near me. "I saw you naked as a baby, and I don't really care to anymore," she told me. I finally "ripped off the Band-Aid," and closed my eyes to pretend—like a two year old—that if I couldn't see anyone, then no one could see me. As I heard a helicopter flying overhead, I prayed no one was taking aerial photographs.

I auditioned for *Survivor*, went on a raid with a SWAT team and vice squad, and crashed both a wedding and a fraternity party. I endured fearful, awkward, and embarrassing moments in nearly all of my fifty-two ventures.

As I shared these escapades—and heard from readers living vicariously yet far more safely through them—I learned most of us have very *narrow* comfort zones. Those comfort zones get even tighter as we grow older.

This is especially true for women: since we've been taught from a very young age to not take risks. This includes avoiding situations that not only could physically harm us but that also might frighten or embarrass us. I mean, why would we do anything that might prove awkward or humiliating—which might lead to people laughing at us —*on purpose?*

Yet each time I survived another new and sometimes excruciating experience, I felt less nervous and more self-assured. Because going outside our safety zone ultimately *empowers* us. We learn how to live with humility. We gain confidence. And, even if we seem to fail at some attempt, we succeed just by putting ourselves out there.

At some point, we may even discover the most rewarding experiences in life are those we've been sidestepping all along.

By taking on this "unbucket list," I changed my life. I learned a great deal about the world around me and about myself. Above all, I *finally* learned to laugh at myself.

I discovered that finding humor in difficult situations is perhaps the *best* reaction of all.

I seldom worry anymore about facing new challenges or potentially embarrassing circumstances. Few experiences turn out as we expect anyway. So, why spend our time or energy worrying? You experience a huge rush of freedom the first time you let something roll off your shoulders.

If an experience does happen to go *way* downhill—let's say, if you manage to destroy the lobby of a Segway rental shop during your inaugural ride? Or, if you find yourself unable to face your perfectionist salon technician during your first Brazilian wax? The ability to laugh at yourself in the *worst* imaginable of predicaments manages to help ease the pain—or at least the emotional sting.

My year of crazy new experiences proved to be fear-fueled, fun, and unbelievably self-satisfying. And it didn't result in just 52 weeks of crazy challenges. It changed me—and my life—forever.

I still find great joy in making others laugh. It's forever rewarding to discover people laughing *with* me.

Yet the new me now faces awkward situations with far less concern about how others will react to my success or my failure. Damn if I won't find a way to laugh at the outcome, even if people are actually laughing *at* me. And *that* happens pretty frequently.

By exposing ourselves to uncomfortable situations, we grow a bit stronger and more confident. We find a way to laugh at nearly anything —even if we happen to be the butt of the joke.

If I could travel back in time to that junior high program in my school basement, I'd probably still feel mortified as I tooted louder than the brass section in an orchestra.

But this time, I'd laugh, stand up in the middle of the heckling crowd, and shout, "Thank you! Thank you very much! I'm still mastering the trumpet. But give me a drumroll, and I'll toot even louder!"

Yes, learning to laugh at yourself is one helluva survival tactic.

If you gain the self-assurance to laugh at yourself, you may discover that the crowd will laugh along with you.

Life is funny that way.

SHERRY STANFA-STANLEY *IS AN AWARD-WINNING WRITER, humorist, and squeamish adventurer. Her memoir,* Finding My Badass Self: A Year of Truths and Dares, *chronicles her insane and enlightening year of misadventures. Sherry's work appears in* The Rumpus, Healthy Aging, First for Women, *and* The Huffington Post, *and in the anthologies* Fifty Shades of Funny *and* Laugh Out Loud. *An empty-nester, she now indulges a menagerie of badly behaved pets.*

❧ 9 ❧

RISE UP

BY KATELYN SULLIVAN

Rise up
When you're living on your knees you
Rise up
Tell your brother that he's gotta
Rise up
Tell your sister that she's gotta
Rise up

— HAMILTON

HAMILTON HAS ALWAYS BEEN A STEADY BEAT IN THE BACKGROUND OF my life. I can rap along with Angelica and Hamilton, beatbox and sing with Eliza, and have learned a bit of French from Lafayette. Lin-Manuel Miranda has recreated Alexander Hamilton's life to a backdrop of pop music. Most people listen to *Hamilton* because it's catchy and entertaining, but the meanings behind the words can really teach people amazing life lessons.

In *My Shot*, Alexander tells of how he's dreamed of America, and his ambitions about the new country. Later, his newfound friend John Laurens raps about how, no matter what happens, you have to fight back, rise up, and get back in the game with even more insistence. People all around me my entire life have been telling me the same life lesson. No matter what happens, fight back. Stand up for yourself, and stand up for your peers.

My sisters and mother have been telling me the same thing. I've gone to a D.C. Women's March, and been educated about the importance of equality, equal pay, ending stereotyping, and treating others the same as you want to be treated. Growing up in a wonderful family, I've almost never felt unsafe, insecure, or distressed. And I wish I could make it so everyone felt the same way as I do. Although, at a time, I did understand what some people go through —bullying.

I'm female, unusually tall, and white, with chestnut hair I wear loose around my neck. A braided hair tie is almost always around my right wrist, and dusty blue glasses are pushed up against the bridge of my nose, hiding aqua eyes and long lashes. Nearly 13, but I always look older, shoulders slightly slumped so I look an inch shorter—not that it makes any difference to my towering figure.

When I first transferred to my current school in third grade, I was elated. Both my sisters had gone to this school, and met all their best friends there. I was familiar with the teachers, and I knew the layout of the school better than my old one. I didn't realize that sometimes it isn't all fun and games.

When I first met him, I immediately noticed he was sporty and popular. First impressions aren't always the end product though. He was intimidated by me, most likely because I was at least a head taller than him. Being a third-grader, feelings were hurt easily. He'd just have to glare over his shoulder, make a snarky comment to one of my friends, or not talk to someone for a day, and *WHAM*—half the class was in tears.

I'd come home everyday, eyes livid with the pain of his new, sharp insults. I'd ignore my family's worried glances and go up to my room, burying myself in a book until bedtime. One day, when my mother came in to drop off my instrument, the bully had delivered an especially rude insult. All I'd tried to do was explain that I used to own a snake while he and his friends were talking about reptiles.

"Aaron! Aaron!" I'd excitedly burst in. "You used to have a snake? Me too! Her name was Nagini, after Voldemort's in Harry Potter, and—"

"You're just as much a snake as the one you used to own!" He'd hissed with the likeness of a serpent, then lifting his chin in the air and whirling back around.

I've always prided myself on being able to handle tough situations, but this was a bit too much for nine-year-old me to handle. I burst into tears. And to make it worse, I cried in front of my mother and my entire class. I was rushed to the counselor's office for an entire hour.

It continued on like this for a year, until, thank goodness, fourth grade arrived. This boy wasn't put into my class, which lifted a weight off my shoulders. That lasted for about five minutes. His tormenting was the worst that year. At any given time he'd find me and my friends and verbally attack us.

But that wasn't even the worst part—sometimes Aaron would be nice, and would talk to me like we were old pals. He'd play with my friends at recess, sit with us at lunch. It would be a peaceful, blissful few days for the entire class when he was kind. But once Monday came back around, he was back to his old insults.

The next year—fifth grade—was also different, though. I had the best teacher anyone could ask for, and she didn't tolerate this bully's nonsense. The teacher encouraged my friends and I stand up for ourselves, and by the end of the year the bully had moved to a different school district. Sort of surprisingly, the bully did start being a bit kinder to everyone just before he left.

I haven't really experienced intense bullying, just a somewhat childish type. Aaron never physically hurt me, or threatened me, he just made my life miserable every chance he got for almost three years. Bullying is still bullying, no matter who does it, how old you are, and where it happens. I'll never forget this boy. If I saw him in public, I'd just ignore him and move on with my day. But I will never, *ever* forget that if I hadn't risen up, I might still be unhappy and under his reign.

I've moved past the bully and his antics, and forward into the wonderful new life I lead. I continue to enjoy listening to *Hamilton*, and following more of Lin-Manuel's amazing advice, rapped through the Founding Fathers. I write, read, and draw, with only normal worries on my mind—homework, tests, and sports—instead of the old worries of what would come with tomorrow.

ALOHA! I'M KATELYN SULLIVAN, AND I WROTE THIS PIECE WHEN I was in the sixth grade. I live outside of Washington, D.C., with my family and a suspicious cat and a sweet dog. I'm a Cadette Girl Scout, and I enjoy horseback riding (although I don't get to do it as often as I'd like!), writing, reading, drawing, and listening to Hamilton, *among other things. I'm a very adventurous person, and competed in the Odyssey of the Mind World Finals in Ames, Iowa, in fourth grade, as Aristotle the Eagle. I feel so lucky to have this writing opportunity, and would like to thank everyone who helped make this book possible!*

✺ 10 ✺

BE YOU!

BY TRACY HARGEN

Growing up as girl in the '70s I was always the peacemaker—which meant that at times I changed myself to make others comfortable or to fit it. As an adult, I became an advocate for girls—and it's my mission to spread the word to all girls that they should be themselves. Don't change for anyone and be proud of who you are!

Although I don't have a daughter, I am one and know what it's like to be a young woman in this world. I'm raising two sons and one of my main goals in raising them was I wanted them to become men who aren't intimidated by strong women and who are good men and good partners. Their father set a great example by the way he treats me—their mom. Once you know what is important to you, you need to be sure that whomever you choose to share your life with embodies these things. For me it is thoughtful gestures big and small, respect and most importantly—unconditional love. Think about what it is for you. The single most important thing is for you to be YOU—once you commit to that, everything will fall into place.

In my lifetime of experiences, this is what I've learned about being a woman in the world today—and what I wish I knew when I was growing up:

1. Don't dim your light for anyone. Not your family, not your friends, and certainly not for a guy. Anyone who finds someone else attractive who "plays dumb" or downplays their accomplishments and gifts is competing with you, not loving you. When someone loves you, they want you to excel and they love you for who you are. They do not feel threatened by you—they feel inspired—they want to do better and be better.

You don't need to be "somebody else's something." You don't need to be treated as princess or strive only to be "Daddy's girl" or someone's girlfriend. You will go much further in life (and be infinitely happier) when you own your power and stand in your own light. You don't need anyone else—you can choose someone else if you want to, but stand on your own first and foremost before you invite someone else in. My Mom drilled it into me that you must be able to support yourself before you can get married. You don't want to be stuck in a relationship because you have no alternative. "Stay because you want to, not because you have to." Find someone who supports your dreams and wants you to support theirs—don't become someone you're not so that others feel more comfortable. There are plenty of men who love strong women—and strong women can stand on their own. So go out there and be your best, do your best, because you are more than enough just the way you are!

2. Jealousy does not equal love! When he is jealous, tells you how to dress, and constantly finds fault with you then says, "No one will ever love you the way I do." Believe him—he means it, but not in the way you think. I promise you this, you don't want to be "loved" this way. He may come across as attentive and caring at first but when you're not allowed to think for yourself or be yourself, you are entering dangerous territory.

This controlling behavior will escalate slowly over time until you find yourself conforming for someone else. And when you get fed up and try to stop it, this change will not be welcome. In fact, someone may try to enforce their ways to keep you the way they want. Run! Run fast and far. He won't shove or hit you the first time but he'll make it clear that you need to "get in line." If you've found yourself in this situation, ask for help and take seriously any threats he makes. You've just stood your ground, and that will seem threatening. When a guy really loves you, he loves you for who you are, not how you look standing next to him or how he thinks you should be. A real guy is confident in himself and is not threatened by you talking to the people you choose to talk to, wearing what you want, speaking your mind, and standing on your own. A real man doesn't want to control you or compete with you—he wants you to shine!

3. It's okay not to be okay. If you'd asked me to describe myself growing up I would have said "positive, upbeat, and happy." I'm a "glass half full" kind of gal and see the good in most situations so being happy was easy for me. I was kind to others and empathetic—in how I spoke to them and how I treated them.

I was not always so kind to myself. I held myself to standards that no one could achieve. I was determined and persistent and saw my ambition and striving as some of my stronger qualities—and they were —when they were in check. But I also saw every flaw and every mistake, and those terrified me. I saw them as weaknesses to be conquered. In my mind, I was never smart enough, thin enough, pretty enough, accomplished enough—I could and should always try harder. The kindness I showed others I didn't necessarily show myself. And when all of this striving for perfection and clearly unattainable goals exhausted me and crippled me with fear and anxiety, I had no clue how to ask for help. So I just kept pushing through it—never learning coping mechanisms until I was an adult who was terrified to fly in a plane and was paralyzed with a fear of making a bad decision, certain it would ruin me. Ugh—it was a terrible way to live (all while acting like I was sailing through life without a care in the world.)

So, please, know that it is okay not to be okay. It's okay to make honest mistakes. It's okay not to be perfect—in fact, it's impossible to be perfect so don't do that to yourself. Once you talk to yourself in the caring way to talk to others, you'll be so much happier. Tell that negative voice in your head that you won't allow it to rule your life. Tell it that it can be very cruel, and that is not okay with you anymore. Then talk to yourself the way you would to your best friend when they are struggling. People can't relate to someone who is "perfect"—they relate to someone is human who makes mistakes and forgives themselves. If you're feeling down, or fearful and can't brush it off, ask for help and listen to those who love you—accept their kindness and their love. You'll be amazed how much people are willing to help you when you just ask.

4. Always follow your heart. You know what it feels like—that "gut instinct," that feeling that something feels right or wrong. When you're in a situation and you know instinctively the right thing to do, do it. If you've been taught to doubt yourself—by a parent, sibling, teacher, friend—if you've been taught that your opinion doesn't matter (or worse, that your opinion is "stupid"), you must stop listening to those outside voices. I've made decisions in my life that people responded to with, "You're crazy!" You know what, it might have been a crazy decision for them, but not for me. I'm not a risk-taker but eloped with my husband of 29 years after knowing him for only six months. I know that does seem crazy but I was 23 years old, had a career, could support myself, and was deeply in love. We both knew it was right for us—and we were right! I'm not advocating marrying someone so quickly, but I'm saying that in my heart, I knew it was absolutely right.

I've taken leaps of faith in my life not with my eyes closed, blind to the risks, but with eyes wide open after evaluating the options—and then following my heart. I've hired people, helped people, taken jobs, left jobs, taken chances throughout my life by relying on my instincts. I distinctly remember walking the city streets when my sons were a baby and a toddler. A man passed us who gave me the creeps the way he looked at us. My older son, while holding my hand tightly, moved in closer to me without saying a word and then looked up to me as if to say, "I feel like something is wrong." Once we were safely in the store, I looked at him and said, "That weird feeling in your stomach—it told you something was wrong and made you move closer to me for protection – that's your gut instinct – always listen to it. It will always tell you the right thing to do." If you've ever felt like, "Hmm, something doesn't feel right in this situation," or, "That explanation just doesn't make sense to me," that is your gut or your heart telling you the truth. We all have it, we just have to listen to it—don't try to squelch it or blow it off as "just a

44

feeling"—it's real and it's there for you. Trust it—it's the best guide you have!

5. Being kind beats being pretty any day of the week. I know, what girl doesn't want to be called beautiful? Yes, it's superficial but somehow we've been ingrained to strive for this in a way that guys just don't. It's "the ultimate compliment." Or is it? When I was young I entered a teen beauty pageant. (Hey, it was the '80s in the South—what can I say?!) I wanted that crown and the ginormous trophy that went with it—and if I'm honest, I also wanted proof that I was pretty. What I got was "Miss Congeniality." (I didn't even know it was a thing.)

Don't get me wrong, these were nice girls, but this was a beauty pageant after all and for some of these girls and their moms it was a way of life. After all, we were asking people to look at us as we paraded around and to judge us for how pretty we presented ourselves on the outside. When I saw the other girls had stylists, makeup artists and hairdressers, I should have realized I didn't stand a chance. I'll admit the competition for Miss Congeniality wasn't that tough—I was the only girl there who would rather make new friends then steal someone's makeup. (Yes, that happened.) It took me years to understand that the tiny trophy I received was not the "consolation prize"—it was The Real Prize. A prize that my husband found about 25 years ago in a box of my things. He's proudly displayed it on a shelf in our room ever since. I love that! Being pretty is not sustainable – being kind is who you are at the core. Being pretty serves no purpose - being kind not only feels good to you, it also feels good to all those you come in contact with. So please, choose being kind over being pretty any day of the week. As my dad used to say, "Beauty is only skin deep but ugly is down to the bone." Cruelness, spitefulness, jealousy—those are all ugly, and ugly is hard to change so don't let it ever take root. Be kind—the world needs more kindness.

Now go out there and shine! If they don't accept you, take your light and your power and go shine somewhere else. I promise you this —there are good things ahead for you as long as you are true to yourself and stand in your power. *You are amazing just the way you are so be YOU!*

TRACY HARGEN IS A SOUTHERN GIRL BORN AND BRED WHO DID A stint in the North after meeting her Yankee husband! With their sons out of the house, they're empty-nesters with two beloved pups.

Tracy has worked in Corporate America for over 30 years, but her passions are writing and removing the shame and stigma around mental health issues. Her family's deeply personal journey with depression was featured on CBS This Morning. Look for her work on GrownandFlown.com and LoveWhatMatters.com.

❦ 11 ❦

I KNOW YOU ARE, BUT WHAT AM I: CONFESSIONS FROM A CHILDHOOD BULLY

BY HARPER KINCAID

Okay, let me start by stating the obvious: I couldn't have picked a more unsympathetic topic if I tried. I mean, seriously, if my goal was to have you like me, confessing I used to be a bully is a ridiculous strategy.

If it's any consolation, my bullying tenure was short: it was only for a month during sleep-away camp. By the way, that was also the first and last time I could ever count myself as one of the "cool kids."

Anyway, it was the summer of 1982, when almost everything clicked.

I had a cute boyfriend, an avid tennis player who matched his sweat bands with the colored rubber bands on his braces. Trust me, in the early '80s, that was smoking hot, especially if he sported a Members Only jacket to complete the ensemble.

Also, by some miracle, I made the cheerleading squad, which, considering I couldn't even do a cartwheel, should illuminate all you need to know about the competition. Watching us during try-outs was like witnessing a group of freshly clubbed Nancy Kerrigans return to the ice.

It was painful and *so*-not-pretty.

The girls in Bunk Nine ranged in age from 11 to 13, which meant we were all getting our periods around the same time (many for the first time) while having to listen to The J. Geils Band and a newly sober Elton John. In short, we were living through a level of Hell not ever imagined in Dante's Inferno. We got stuck inside more often than not because it rained almost every day—and there's only so many rounds of jacks to play, or letters on your favorite unicorn and rainbows stationary you can write home with, until people start to crack.

Her name was Susan. In a cabin filled with knobby-kneed awkwardness, she had more than the rest of us, but that's not what made her a target. She was a whiner—about everything—and would speak in a baby voice while tattling on us to the counselors. She also hated anything athletic. None of us were going to be recruited for the all-star team of any sport, but enthusiasm counted. So did grit—two things she had none of.

All that was bad, but what was worse was her affection for her Cabbage Patch doll: Miss McSnuggleMuffins. I swear, I wish I was making this up. That was her name. It was even on that Cabbage Patch birth certificate that came in the box, which was a shame because that creepy doll would be the only one I'd ever want to deport. Keep the immigrants—send back all the dolls.

None of us could believe that, at almost 13 years old, she still had one of those things, saying she couldn't sleep without it. But she didn't just sleep with it; she brought the doll to activities outside the cabin too, at least until the counselors put their foot down.

Looking back, Susan Holly was probably just holding on to childhood a bit longer and harder than the rest of us, but in the late '70s, early '80s, there was no room for such macro-lensed sensitivities. Her eccentricities made her a target. Most teased her, but soon, even that grew dull.

So, one night, when she was out of the cabin, my friend and I stole her Cabbage Patch doll, tied a shoelace around her neck, and hung her off the shower curtain rod with a note attached, saying, "I'd rather die than be with you a minute more. You smell and you're weird."

The next morning, when she returned and found her doll, we all woke up to her screams. She screamed like a SAG actor on a *Law &*

Order show. Everyone laughed, including the counselors. I thought it was hysterical, until she ran by and I saw she was actually crying.

I bet you're hoping this is the part of the story when I finally grow a conscience and rectify my bad behavior, right? Sorry, pookie—at this point, I'm still a little asshole. In fact, I enjoyed a swell of mean girl popularity that made me higher than snorting Pixie Stick sugar off a hooker's ass.

By the way, my friend and I endured a scolding that only lasted a minute and a half, and there was no follow-up punishment. How's that for negative reinforcement?

I know I am telling this story with attempted humor. It's my favorite coping mechanism, but trust me, I look back and cringe at my behavior. Actually, I do more than cringe: I experience a profound sense of shame, horrified I was the architect of someone else's suffering and trauma. It would have been bad enough if I had followed along some other mean girl's nefarious agenda. But the McSnuggle-Muffins *coup d'etat* was my Damian-incarnated brainchild. Even though what happened was my sole improv stint as a Heathers-incarnate, I have to live with the knowledge I was capable of such callousness. But that's not the end of the story.

Ironically, before—and after—the Cabbage Patch Incident—I would deal with my own share of mean girls. Not enough to scar me, but enough to show me how awful it was to be on the other end. I thought that was enough to balance the karmic scales. I was wrong.

Flash forward 20-odd years later. My older daughter is enrolled in preschool and, because she's my first, I'm there all the time, volunteering for a million jobs instead of working one for pay, much to the chagrin of my husband. Since we were living in Miami Beach at the time, my husband and I were near where we grew up, which meant we were constantly bumping into people from various stages of our lives. So, in my daughter's preschool class, it was not unusual that I would've recognized many faces: some from elementary school, others from summer jobs. But there's this one mom who looks familiar, but I can never quite place how I know her.

After six months, I finally figured it out: it's it was Susan. She looked almost the same as she did when she was a 12-year-old camper, which means meant she was one of those kids with an older face early on, so you get the mental picture, but moving on. I don't know why it took me so long to put it together, but it did. Anyway, she's now a hot-shot lawyer surgeon married to another hot-shot lawyer surgeon and has one son—who's adorable, by the way. I can tell she has had no idea who I am, but it's not like I can blame her. Back in our camp days, I was rocking a mouthful of braces, an over-processed perm, circa 1982—complete with Sun-In "highlights" which added a lovely greenish hue in the right light, thanks to the ammonium thioglycolate.

But she does not recognize me. In short, she didn't have a clue who I was. We were all grown up, we were friendly, always smiling at one another and doing the small talk thing during drop-off.

If I wanted, I could be home free. I could keep my newly unearthed knowledge all to myself, with her none the wiser. And hey, she was obviously happy and successful now, maybe what happened wasn't a big deal after all.

I didn't want to bring it up. I wanted to forget all about it, which of course meant I couldn't.

So, I worked up the courage one day, pulled her aside and told her who I was and that I had been the one to hang her doll. The face of the confident woman in front of me fell. She was back to being that almost 13-year-old girl. I felt terrible and so did she.

And so, I did what I should have done years ago. I gave her an earnest, contrite apology. I told her I was sorry for causing her any pain, especially in such an insensitive and graphic way.

Then she asked me why I did it—why did I pick on her? The truth was, she was an easy target. She was out of step with the rest of the groupthink, holding onto regressive behaviors not socially acceptable. But there was no way I was going to say all that. For one thing, I didn't want to blame the victim, even if there may have been kernels of truth to my analysis.

And more importantly, she wasn't looking for truth—she was looking for validation and it was my job to give her what she needed to heal. So, I offered a half-truth—that by picking on her, I avoided getting picked on myself.

After that, she was civil, but basically avoided me if she could help it. I deserved that. Actually, I deserved a lot worse. I had gotten a little bit of power and I abused it, because someone was different and out-of-step—or as hella-hipster-musician, hella-hipster-cool, Beck, would have said: "In a world of chimpanzees, she was the monkey," meaning she was flagging behind on the perceived, socio-evolutionary scale. But the point wasn't to make me feel better, it was to make her feel better. And, like many other things in my life, I failed at that goal as well. I still think people should apologize when they do wrong, own up to their crap, but I'm also of the belief the apology is more for the sinner than the victim.

Ironically, a few years later, I had the opportunity to be someone else's Susan. My former high school nemesis-slash-perpetrator of mean girl nastiness tracked me down to apologize for all of her therapy-worthy torment. She is actually a good friend of mine today, but back during The Many Apologies (which I swear she did, like the first 10 times we saw one another socially) she was tormented by how she had treated me. I decided to ask her the same thing Susan Holly had asked me: "Why me?" She said she didn't know. Maybe she remembered, but didn't want to hurt my feelings. I remember me back then and I was a hot mess. I gossiped. I lied. I was like a walking *ABC Afterschool Special* of everything not to do.

Today, I have two daughters and I have shared my stories of being bullied and being the mean girl. They were horrified, as they should have been. I have taught them to not take crap from anyone and to stand up to such injustices when they witness them. I tell them being kind means more to us than being the top of the class or popular.

When I worked as a school social worker intern during grad school, most of the anti-bullying efforts focused on mediation between bullies, perpetrators, and victims. I'll give you the short version: They didn't work. It was my job to bring together two kids who despised one another and to somehow conjure a sort of social-scientific Kumbaya miracle between recess and lunch. I'll cut to the punchline: It never worked.

The methodology and vernacular may have changed, but bad behavior rarely does. So I did what every grad student does: I scoured the latest research on bullying prevention, because us nerd-girl goobers get off on charts and longitudinal studies.

But who was I deluding? Professional curiosity was not the only motivator: the Susans were. Except now some of the Susans may feel more like Stephens inside. And maybe some of the Susans and Stephens want to be accepted for being Sams, something fluid and uniquely in between. I graduated with a masters in Gender History in the early 2000s and most of today's gender identifiers didn't even exist back then. So, maybe our collective, myopic lenses are widening.

However, while being able to identify with one's tribe is a critical component towards self-hood, such actualizations do not eliminate the problem. While researching for effective anti-bullying initiatives, I am happy to share that there are programs that have proven effective. In Finland, they have something called the KiVa program. It is a pre-K through twelfth grade, anti-bullying curricula which alters entire school cultures against intimidating behavior. Apparently, without a supportive audience, it seems bullying conduct fizzles out before it ignites. The KiVa program is not fool-proof, but studies over the last several years have shown statistically significant results in lowered aggressive behaviors.

Imagine if such a curriculum had existed at my summer camp, that the minute someone realized I had grabbed Susan's doll and wrote that note, the entire cabin would have turned on me. Maybe someone would have come up and said, "This is not who we are or what we do." Imagine that.

I still insist on the importance of self-awareness and personal responsibility. But having one's community set us right is also appealing. And although this alternate scenario sounds like an unrealistic dream to me, it is a reality in Finland. Of course, last I heard, Finland also has the highest suicide rates in the world, but I think that's due more to living in perpetual winter with lots of vodka, but what do I know?

In all seriousness, such programs and studies give me hope, especially in our country's divided socio-political environment, with bullying behavior on both sides of the aisle. For a country so passionate about God, we are all in serious need of a come-to-Jesus moment. We have to try something different to go beyond our standard modus operandi, of only working with victims and perpetrators.

Because it doesn't work. It has *never* worked.

Maybe it's too late for us aging and jaded Gen Xers (I don't believe that), but it isn't for the next generation. What I do believe, with everything I am, is in the power of grace and redemption. Personal responsibility, accountability, and collective kindness are the values which can truly save us. I know this to be true because they saved me.

BORN IN CALIFORNIA AND RAISED IN SOUTH FLORIDA, HARPER KINCAID moved around like a gypsy with a bounty on her head. She's been a community organizer and a professional matchmaker. Ms. Kincaid is a published author, known mostly for her romantic comedies, such as The Wonder of You *and her new release,* Love in Real Life. *She also writes creative nonfiction, poetry, and, most recently, cozy mysteries and suspense.*

She is a self-admitted change junkie, but is now happily settled in the cutest 'lil town of Vienna, Virginia, with her wife-whisperer husband, and their two girls.

✿ 12 ✿

SOME DAYS

BY KATY FARBER

Some days
I show up in the world
like an open wound
ready to bleed
for whoever wants me to
apologizing for whatever it is
I haven't said yet
whatever you need
whatever you did
or didn't do
I'll take the blame
fill in the blank
for not enough...
mothering
listening
care-taking
being quiet silence
being compliant compliance

I'll bleed apology

before you even open
your mouth.

Other days
I show up so angry
my blood boils
at every indignity
of the female kind
at every glossy representation
of who I will never be
at every subtle way
the world tells me to be
pretty
friendly
happy
smart but not too smart
enjoying the male gaze
having it all!
while making less than men
again and again
while being interrupted
questioned
silenced
again and again
until I remind myself
to breathe
and turn away.

Other days
I'm so gaslit
I'm so confused
by the world
by the news
by the reality
that I think
I must be

what's wrong
it must be me
losing my mind
slow but surely
unraveling like
a ball of tightly
wound string.

Other days
I feel the power
of one woman
who tells her story
and she is heard
and how it helps
another woman
tell her story
and bit by bit
they share the truth
the often messy
complicated
imperfect truth
of female lives
and I feel that we
just might be
making progress
and in the very least
I am not alone.

Some days
as a woman
in America, 2018.

KATY FARBER is an educator, researcher and author who lives in Vermont with her husband and daughters. She has books published across genres including education and middle grade fiction. Her most recent book is a picture book called *Salamander Sky,* which was a finalist for the New England Book Award. She regularly writes about education, the environment, parenting, and current issues for various websites, journals, and blogs. Learn more and connect at katyfarber.com or on Twitter at @Non_Toxic_Kids.

13

DEAR DAUGHTER, YOU ARE ENOUGH

BY DEVA DALPORTO

Dear Daughter,

You are enough.

You are enough just as you are. You don't have to be prettier or faster or smarter or sparklier or cooler or quieter or smaller or perkier or smilier or stronger or anything other than what you are. Because you are enough.

I see you comparing yourself. To me. To your friends. To your brother. To random people you'll never know.

I see you putting yourself down. Telling yourself you aren't good enough. Staring at your reflection in the mirror with critical eyes as you brush your hair and wish it were silkier. Putting yourself down for running the fastest mile in your P.E. class, but not the fastest mile in your school. Ripping up your art because it's not quite as good, in your eyes, as one your friend drew.

I see you deflecting credit for great accomplishments and beating yourself up for perceived failures. I see you expecting yourself to be perfect. And I want to scream,

DO NOT DO THIS TO YOURSELF.

Because let me tell you, baby girl, there will be so many people in this life that will try to rip you down. So many others who will judge you and try to make you feel small so they can feel big.

DO NOT DO IT TO YOURSELF.

Do not buy into the script the world serves us girls at birth. That we are not enough. Not pretty enough. Or thin enough. Or strong enough. Or quiet enough. Or worth enough to make the same amount of money as a man who does the same exact job as we do.

It's time for that script to be rewritten.

You don't have to be perfect to be enough. There's no such thing as perfect. Perfect is BS. We are all flawed, every one of us, and that's what makes us interesting. If it existed, perfect would be boring.

But what you do have to be is accepting. Of yourself. Of your flaws. Of your strengths. Of your "You-ness." You have to be your own greatest champion. You have to take credit for your greatness. You have to believe in your awesomeness. You have to be as strong and brave and loud and big as you really are. Do not dull yourself for anyone.

Shine.

I want you to see yourself for the glorious, magnificent, kick-ass creature you truly are.

And I want you to always remember,

YOU ARE ENOUGH.

Just as you are.

Love,
Mom

DEVA DALPORTO OF MYLIFESUCKERS IS THE CREATOR OF DOZENS OF viral videos. She is known primarily for her funny music parody videos for which NBC dubbed her the "Weird Al of YouTube Moms." Her videos have garnered more than 300 million views and have been on Good Morning America, The Today Show, People, CNN, NBC, ABC, Good House-keeping, *and many more. Deva is a three-time BlogHer Voice of the Year*

Award winner for video, an Iris Award winner for Best Parenting Videos, and was selected by ABC News as "Best Fan Cover Artist" in their Billboard Music Awards Special. *She has essays in two Jen Mann anthologies* I Just Want to Be Alone *and* I Just Want to Be Perfect. *Deva blogs at MyLife-Suckers.com and you can find her on YouTube, Instagram, and Facebook.*

14

DEAR MOM, YOU ARE ENOUGH

BY A.M. DALPORTO

Dear Mom,

You are enough.

You don't have to be the perfect mom. You don't have to be stronger or softer or kinder or craftier or make more organic meals.

I see you beat yourself up whenever you raise your voice. You don't have to be perfectly calm all the time.

I see you disappointed when you don't have everything under control. You don't have to do it all alone.

I see you calling yourself out of shape and criticizing your body. But your "muffin top" just shows that you created two children. And that's pretty cool.

I see you saying you're getting old and staring at your wrinkles in the mirror. And that's true. Everyone is getting older. But the older you get, the wiser you are and the more beautiful you become. Because your marks and lines are memories of your life.

I see you worrying that everybody is better than you, but if you really think about it, nobody is better than anyone else. We're all special in our own way.

You think everything you do for us has to be a masterpiece. But that's not true. If everything was perfect nothing would be special.

You think you have to do it all—the cooking, the cleaning, the cuddling, the planning, the packing, the picking up, the dropping off, the helping with homework—and actually, you do have to do it all. Without you, we wouldn't survive a week. So give yourself some credit.

Even though you're a mom, it's okay to be human. And have flaws. You don't have to be perfect.

YOU ARE ENOUGH.

Just as you are.

Love,
Your Daughter

A.M. DALPORTO IS 12 YEARS OLD. SHE'S ALWAYS HAD A LOVE FOR writing and dreams of becoming an author. She creates humorous videos with her family on their channel MyLifeSuckers and has written a few of her own parodies. She is currently working on her first children's book and is very excited to be included in this anthology.

❧ 15 ❧

AUDITION SHIRT

BY JANEL MILLS

I found my audition shirt on one of my many shopping trips to Salvation Army during high school. It was a blue gingham, button-up blouse with short sleeves, a Peter Pan collar trimmed with eyelet lace, and bright red cherries hand-embroidered along and in between the top buttons. It was an anomaly in my closet, hanging next to my faded second-hand t-shirts and oversized flannels, this ultra-feminine, slim-fitting blouse. It was my secret weapon, my red herring, my invisible sucker punch straight to the gut.

❧

DRUMLINE IS A BOY'S CLUB. I'VE BEEN IN MANY DIFFERENT drumlines over the years, in a few different organizations, and in each line I can count on one hand the number of female members. I guess there could be a lot of reasons for that. For starters, the whole point of drums is to bang on something very hard and make very loud noises, and if you've ever once spent an hour with a two-year-old boy, you know that this in and of itself is like a siren song for testosterone. In addition, you don't generally see girls being steered towards percussion in beginning band classes. Also, real talk: The equipment is *heavy*. The lightest piece of equipment starts at about 30 pounds, and it just goes up from there. So yeah, it's a tough sell for most girls physically, and keep in mind, you're trying to sell the idea of carrying something extremely heavy not to athletes, but to girls like me who may or may not have signed up for multiple music classes specifically to avoid taking gym class.

Despite the heavy drum and being suckered into playing the oboe in junior high (arguably the most obnoxious instrument of all), I decided that I needed to join the marching band, and my route to do that was going to be the drumline. Several of my good friends were already members, and served as my ambassadors to the existing drum tech when early winter practices and tryouts began. The tech soon discovered that my friends were right about me: I was tough, I wasn't a complainer, and I could read and learn music pretty damn well. I picked up the smallest bass drum on the first night, and after five minutes, I was sold. Drumming became my passion: it was my thing, and I loved everything about it.

After about a year and a half, three of my friends in the line and I decided we wanted to try out for a winter drumline. Winter drumline is when drumlines compete against each other during the off-season, playing music and marching around gymnasiums. While the bigger, richer high school across town had a winter line, our school, which was less than flush with cash, didn't have one. Somehow, one of us (to this day, I have no idea how we did this, as it was before the dawn of the Internet) figured out that there was a newly formed winter drumline in a rich suburb about an hour away that was holding open auditions. We jumped in the car after school and drove there, ready to kill this audition.

What I failed to realize, however, was that the reason I had never been bothered by being one of the only girls in my high school's drumline was because I had basically grown up with nearly every single member of our tiny line. They knew me already, so my gender wasn't an issue. I quickly realized that outside of my little comfort zone of familiarity, these new drummer dudes were going to assume certain qualities about me, including:

- Can't read music very well
- Only joined the drumline because they ran out of percussionists
- Will constantly ask to set down her drum because she can't handle the weight
- Has no chops (i.e., hand/arm muscle strength, which enables you to play well and play longer)
- Doesn't possess a penis (this one was true)

I remember feeling more and more annoyed as I got the sense that the person running the bass drum auditions fully believed most, if not all, of these things about me. He gave a shitty, condescending nod when I said I was typically used to playing bass one. This instructor made the fatal mistake of assuming that because I was a girl and only weighed 100 pounds soaking wet, I played that drum because it was the lightest. In fact, I continued playing that drum because it's one of the more technically challenging bass drums in the line; I was playing college-level rudiments and doubling some of the snare drum music.

Big mistake. Huge.

He thought he would be funny and put me on bass two, which is actually the toughest drum to play in a bass line, because your notes constantly fall on the upbeat. I'd never played bass two before, but you know what? Sure. I was working myself up to being pissed, and was more than ready to prove how sorely mistaken this guy was for underestimating me. We started playing the audition music, and it became very clear, very quickly that I was the strongest player in the line. I was catching all of the oddly timed notes the first time through the audition exercise, and the instructor noticed. His attitude changed dramatically after we finished running through that piece. As I straightened back up after setting down my drum for a 10-minute break, I realized I was wearing my silly new gingham shirt with the little red cherries and the eyelet lace. It dawned on me that I had worn the most saccharine-sweet, feminine shirt that I owned to compete against a horde of Y chromosomes.

After that night, I wore my audition shirt any time I had to try out for a new drumline. When I moved on to college and wanted to try out for the drumline at the Big Ten school I was attending, I knew it was a long shot. I knew I was going to deal with the same bullshit I dealt with in other lines – having to prove myself beyond their expectations of female players. However, I still had my secret weapon. It was probably 100 degrees at that first weekend tryout camp, but I still wore that cotton button-up shirt with the Peter Pan collar and the eyelet lace.

Because I had an impression to make.

Because I had false expectations to grab and suddenly shove back into the face of those holding on to them.

I'D LOVE TO TELL YOU THAT I STILL HAVE MY AUDITION SHIRT, THAT I eventually retired it, hanging it from the rafters of my attic in a place of honor like a retired NHL jersey. Sadly, however, I'm not quite sure where it is. It could be in my basement with my other clothes that I can't bear to part with, or I could have returned it from whence it came, tossing it into one of my Goodwill donation boxes once I finally admitted to myself that it doesn't fit, and will never fit me ever again. Either way, it's all good. Even without the shirt, I've held on to the thrill of annihilating people's false expectations of me because of my gender. Was I wearing my cherry shirt the day that pompous judge tried explaining to me, a librarian, how law libraries and legal research works? Nope. I wasn't, but I still smiled while I blasted him with my knowledge of how *modern* legal libraries were set up and managed, including the one that I currently ran. My years of drumline taught me that I'm a bad bitch, to have confidence in the face of doubt, and that even if the men around me don't realize it right away, they will very, very soon.

JANEL MILLS IS THE LIBRARIAN/THUG BEHIND THE BLOG 649.133: Girls, the Care and Maintenance Of, where she writes about raising a princess, a wild child, and the sassiest redhead on Earth using as many curse words as

possible. Janel was a contributor to several super successful anthologies includ-
ing the I Just Want to Pee Alone *series. When not blogging or librarian-ing,*
she keeps busy raising three beautiful little girls in the wilds of metro Detroit.

❧ 16 ❧

MY PENIS MAKE MILK

BY MONICA GOKEY

I was a two-kid kind of person until I had two sons.

By the time my second was six months old, the #MeToo movement had been unfolding in the news for weeks. Personal #MeToo disclosures blossomed across my Facebook feed, making an at-large movement suddenly feel very much at home. It made my heart hurt.

All the men in my life were under fresh scrutiny. I wondered which were the ones I perceived them to be, versus the ones with transgressions under their belts (pun intended). When I did a mental line-up of the men I felt the most positive about, a single trait ran through them like a ribbon: They all had strong women in their lives—awesome moms, stubborn sisters, or kick-ass girlfriends and wives.

Family planning is a pretty shit casino game. You get 50/50 odds the female body of a slot machine deposits you a boy or a girl. But in the wake of #MeToo, I readied myself to run the gauntlet. I signed up for a third pregnancy like it was an Oprah sweepstakes (although the odds of winning were definitely higher). Fifty-fifty isn't too shabby... and every gambler knows the house can't always win.

Ahead of our third baby's arrival, I did my best to brainwash my sons into wishing for a sister. I hyped the girl-wishing to them like we were on the cusp of winning a trip to Disneyland. We're gender-surprise people, so we didn't have a 'big reveal' until the baby made its earthly entry. Everyone in our family had been thoroughly inoculated with "we want a girl" fever.

(For the record, I would've been over the moon with a child of either gender. Babies make you soft that way.)

After 42 weeks of pregnancy (yep, you read that right), an unpleasant day at the hospital, and a flood of mushy-gushy emotions—we *did* end up having a girl. The moment felt huge. I'd been entrenched in boy world for three years, and the arrival of a girl left me feeling like balance had been restored to the proverbial Force.

Behold, household! There are two of us now!

When my sons finally met their sister at the hospital, it was immediately clear to me something was amiss.

"Where's her penis?" the oldest, age three, asked.

"She doesn't have a penis," I explained. "She's a *girl*."

"Why she no have a penis?" he said.

I realized I'd been operating under the blind assumption he *knew* the difference between a boy and a girl. He knew Mama was "a girl," but the details of that label had clearly escaped him.

"Girls don't have penises. They have vaginas... and boobies," I patiently explained.

My three-year-old nodded knowingly.

His little brother, one-and-a-half, just screamed "PENIS!... NOOOOO!" at the decibel level he's used to communicating at.

Both knew about boobies. But "vagina" was new to them. "Gi-nuh? ... GI-NUH... VAHHHH-GI-NUH!!" They tried out the new word with alacrity.

Progress.

I was somewhat blindsided by the fact that they didn't know the mechanics of the boy/girl distinction. We live on a cattle ranch in central Idaho. Ever since their eyes have been open they've seen roosters having their way with chickens, bulls mounting cows, and countless other iterations of "the birds and the bees."

Our daughter's first few weeks were marked by this total lack of gender awareness—which was its own kind of awesome.

The boys didn't understand why our families had gifted us a mountain of severely pink clothing. (I didn't understand either, to be fair.)

Too young to know any foolish adages like "girls don't poop" – they ooh'd and ahh'd at the ferocity of their sister's buttery yellow discharges.

"Wow, dat one so big!" my oldest would cheer.

"Yeah, like a fire hose," I would add as I frantically tried to contain any escaping squirts.

And they didn't hesitate to call her the kind of names they called each other. For the first week they called her Dirt. We put the kibosh on that after worrying family outsiders would think we were living some kind of twisted Cinderella story.

During my daughter's first few weeks, I saw their tiny mental light bulbs flicker with more vigor on the whole boy-girl front.

One morning my 18-month-old was reading in bed with me when the baby needed to nurse. I stopped our book to get her latched on. I clenched my teeth and curled my toes while she chomped on to a sore nipple. My younger son put his chubby hand on my arm in a gesture of comfort.

"Hurt?" he said.

"Yeah, hurt," I replied before resuming our book as the latch-on pain faded.

When the baby was crying, my oldest would offer her the kind of comfort he liked.

"She want a cookie?"

"No, thanks. She just drinks milk," I'd tell him. But mentally I logged his comment as a win for budding empathy skills.

We've always tried to stress the importance of character traits like empathy and kindness to our sons. But it wasn't until having a girl that I started to see those teachings bear fruit. Maybe it has nothing to do with having a girl. Maybe it's just the presence of a mewling, helpless, adorable newborn that encourages our best selves shine forth. Either way, there was a change in our family—more helping, more teamwork, and more understanding between everyone, big and small. Although I'm hardly one to live by the old adage "mother knows best," I can't help but feel like the added feminine presence had something to do with our family synergy.

The she-power soon escalated beyond my wildest dreams.

Monday is the only day I swing an entire shift of stay-at-home mom life. We drive an hour each way to preschool (because it's the kind of thing rural parents do to socialize their kids). On the way to our favorite "apres-pre" burger joint, some heavy conversation rocked the minivan.

My three-year-old told me sadly that Ducky (his stuffed bestie) can't drink milk from a cup. He sighed heavily.

"Can Ducky drink milk from a straw?" I asked.

"No."

Long pause.

"Ducky drink milk from me," he said, perking up.

"Oh, like how Mama feeds Virginia? From your chest?"

OMG this is so cool... he's having boob envy!

"No. Ducky drink milk from my penis."

Oh shit... what the—

"Yeah... my penis make milk."

I internally facepalmed. Three is too young to understand that it's not cool to conjure up the visual of anything sucking from your pecker, not even a stuffed toy duck.

We dropped the conversation and stuffed our faces with burgers and fries when we got to the restaurant. (Restaurants: also a big novelty when you live out in the wop-wops.)

That night when my husband got home from work I told him about our three-year-old's milk-making penis. He laughed, and then gently prodded me to read between the proverbial lines.

"Vern wishes he was like you," my husband said.

"Like me?"

"Yes. Like you," he insisted. "Think about how amazing it is to a kid his age that you can make milk to feed a baby. And all the other things you do."

I internally blushed at the thought... but this line of thought felt right.

In the coming weeks my oldest son would sometimes sigh wistfully and say, "I want to be a girl." Those words made me feel warm and fuzzy inside. The female body is an amazing thing... so much more than a baby-making slot machine. Even a three-year-old gets it.

And the female psyche is pretty amazing, too. I can't speak for all women, but being emotional has always been a pillar of my life. As far as I can tell, it's normal. I may be short-tempered, impatient, and hotheaded—but I'm also deeply loving, committed to my family, and perceptive of other people's emotions. Those traits aren't exclusively female, but I know a lot of kickass, amazing women with similar temperaments. I want my sons to know that all of it is normal. The whole package isn't anything like looks in magazines. (It's way more explosive.)

It probably shouldn't have taken a third kid to ensure my sons grew up acclimated to all-that-is-female. But I like having back-up.

MONICA GOKEY IS A PRINT AND RADIO JOURNALIST IN WEST-central Idaho, where three kids, a cattle ranch, and low-speed internet interfere with her persistent attempts to be a real writer (whatever that means). Her work has aired on public radio stations in the West and Alaska.

❧ 17 ❧

HOW TO BE SHRILL LIKE A PRO

BY SARAH COTTRELL

In 1989, I was in the fifth grade. My teacher, Mr. Brown, was a very stiff British sort of man. He always wore ill-fitting gray wool suits. Every day he would lift up a rogue mitten or scarf and hold it out like it was the most revolting thing he'd ever seen while asking, "To whom does this belong?" He would always drawl out the 'whom' and purse his already puckered up face into a scowl. The top of his head was balding while the sides and back were long and gray—and not a nice gray either, it was more of an elderly mothball gray. He would comb his hair up into a long sausage curl on top of his head.

That curl held a peculiar amount of curiosity with me and my class-mates. So, it wasn't much of a surprise when Tom, the annoying kid who sat perpendicular to me, dared me to stick my finger through Mr. Brown's curl. I did. Mr. Brown was not amused and made a rather loud example of how disrespectful I was. As he pointed at his head—that was now shiny bald since my finger snagged the curl and it all fell down —he stammered out a quick comparison between my inexcusable inso-lence and Michelle, a very polite and quiet girl who always did what she was told. Michelle and I both blushed in embarrassment.

Mr. Brown was boring, for sure, and he may have disliked kids what with the way he spoke to us. But that man, whether he intended to or not, would give me the most potent introduction to feminism that I ever could have asked for. He showed me that being shrill, which apparently meant vocal if you're female, is a gift, not a curse—and to this day it is still my superpower.

One day, Mr. Brown announced that we would break up into four debate teams. He stood in front of the class and held two newspapers, one was national and one was local. He talked about the current events that the general public was debating. Most of it was political but some of it was cultural.

He asked the class to read through each newspaper and identify several topics that we could debate in a friendly classroom competition. By the end of the hour, we had several topics written up on the chalkboard in perfectly illegible fifth-grade writing.

Mr. Brown wrote all the topics on pieces of paper and then added them to a hat. He broke the class into four groups.

I was stuck with the three most irritating boys, Tom, Jason, and Eric. I couldn't stand them and I was dreading this activity. These were the boys who ran up to me during recess and poked me in my back then ran away screaming. They pulled my hair. They teased me incessantly. And no matter how many times my mother told me, "It just means they like you," I was never left with an overwhelming feeling of being respected by them. They were basically jerks.

"And now, each of your groups will choose a team captain," Mr. Brown said while holding back his imaginary British accent.

Of course, I was not chosen. Jason said that he would be the captain. He looked right at me as he explained loudly that boys are natural leaders. I was bored to tears with the classroom exercise that was obviously not meant for me. My three teammates were distracted by talk of wall ball and Jason's new sneakers. I imagined that this was how the boys must have felt during Home Economics class when every activity was clearly invented for girls in order to learn how to run a home. Teachers must have thought that girls weren't capable of ambition beyond learning to sew a button by hand. Middle school was turning out to be hard.

Mr. Brown walked over to our table and offered the hat toward the center of the table. Jason reached in and pulled out a long marigold-yellow piece of paper.

"Ah, I see you'll be debating a classic today. Should women be allowed to play professional basketball?" Mr. Brown was talking to Jason but glanced sideways at me. I couldn't tell, but it felt like he was sending me some kind of message. What, I had no idea.

The boys started talking about basketball. This is a sport that I knew nothing about and to this day I have less than no desire to ever watch a game. But while the boys sat there chewing on details of Michael Jordan and Charles Barkley, I was looking at the clock and realizing that time was running out.

I took out a piece of notebook paper and drew a line down the middle. "Hey, guys, we should really come up with all the reasons why girls can play basketball and reasons why they can't that way we can be ready for whatever the other debate team will throw at us."

Tom rolled his eyes and asked me if I could even spell basketball.

"Um, duh...can you even think of a reason why girls can't play?" I shot back.

The three boys stared at me as I did something that to this day still disturbs me. I listed off all the reasons girls are told that they—that we—aren't capable of playing the same sports as boys. We have periods that make us unstable and crazy. We might bleed to death. We wear distracting clothes and makeup and shoes. We can't run fast because we run like girls. Our long nails will break off if we try to dribble a ball. We are offensively distracting to boys, which is inexplicably unfair to boys. We cat fight. We're dumb. We're weak. We're girls.

Notably, some of those same reasons were given by the public for why couldn't or shouldn't be able to play any sport professionally.

The looks on the boys' faces were incredulous. They didn't seem to think that I should know these reasons. Eric accused me of stealing his ideas, never mind that I was the only one doing any work.

Mr. Brown was quietly watching our group from his oak desk at the front of the classroom. He stood up and smoothed out his necktie before walking over to our cluster of desks that we had pushed together. He perched behind Tom, who was sitting in front of me, crossed his arms and peered down at our group list of pros and cons.

Mr. Brown looked at me and asked how it felt, as the only female in our group, to see and hear all of the negative things listed about girls and women. But before I could answer, Tom said, "Sarah came up with all of the cons and she told us to come up with the pros but we're stuck."

"And you don't think that's odd, Tom?" replied Mr. Brown.

"Why? She was being bossy and took over our whole project! Jason was supposed to be the leader but she started doing all the work," Tom complained.

Mr. Brown looked at me and repeated his original question.

"I feel frustrated and angry that boys are so stupid about fairness when it comes to sports, Mr. Brown," I started. "I'm the third fastest runner in our whole grade and I'm a girl but that doesn't count because I'm a girl. It's a lazy and stupid argument."

My hands shook a little and I remember being quite taken by surprise by how strongly I felt about girls being allowed to play sports. But it was more just that. I was angry about boys feeling like they could speak for me, that they could take over anything from an opportunity to play in sports to a classroom group exercise. I wanted to cry but I knew I my point be lost on these boys if they saw tears.

So, I sucked it up and I looked Mr. Brown right in the eye and I said, "I took over the assignment because no one was working and this needed to get done."

Mr. Brown smiled at me for the first time really ever. It was a warm smile and I felt like something important had just transpired. A sense of power that I had never felt was mine settled into me and I sat a little taller.

I can't say for sure if those boys learned anything that afternoon. And I don't fully recall the eventual debate that we had against an opposing team of classmates, although I do recall the laughter and jeering at my delivering a list of reasons for why girls shouldn't play basketball.

What I do recall, with laser-sharp clarity, is that I felt empowered to use my voice and speak up about an issue that felt squarely unfair. Girls and women may be different than boys and men but they ought to be given equal access to opportunities, power, and influence.

As a woman, I have a voice and I am obliged to use it to question authority and speak out against inequality even if that means upsetting people. As I raise my daughter and two sons, I am hopeful that they will carry this lesson close to their hearts.

SARAH COTTRELL IS A FREELANCE WRITER LIVING IN MID-COAST Maine with her husband and three children. Her work has been widely published online and has been included in six other anthologies including the New York Times *bestselling series* I Still Just Want to Pee Alone. *You can follow Sarah on Facebook under her moniker @housewifeplus.*

DO AS GRANDMA SAYS: RECYCLED ADVICE FOR MY TEENAGE DAUGHTER

BY SUSANNE KERNS

S ince no teenage girl wants to listen to her mom's advice, I've decided to give you someone else's advice instead: Grandma's. She gave me this advice when I was your age, and after decades of testing it out, it ends up she actually knew what she was talking about.

GRANDMA'S GOLDEN RULE: GET A GOOD JOB SO YOU CAN support yourself, and never have to rely on anyone else.

If you want some serious, no-nonsense life advice, talk to a single mom who raised two kids in rural Idaho in the '80s without a college degree. Somehow, she managed to make this advice sound empowering and not all, "*Geez, Mom, I'm only 13, I'm not planning my divorce proceedings quite yet.*" It's still the best advice I've ever received. Over the years, I've seen friends triumph over horrible situations by heeding this advice and I've seen friends' lives crumble due to seemingly minor issues by ignoring it. I may look like "just a stay-at-home mom," but I was able to make that choice because I bought my own house and saved up a nest egg before I even got married. I also always keep one toe in the water so that I could go back to work tomorrow if there was an emergency.

GOLDEN RULE PART B: WORK HARD IN SCHOOL SO YOU CAN GO to a good college in order to get that good job.

This one is a subcategory of the Golden Rule, but I would like to clarify something: A "good" college education depends on what you put into it. You can learn a lot at a $40,000-a-year university or at a $4,000-a-year university. You can also waste a lot of time and money at the same universities. Your time is even more valuable than money— don't squander it. Never again in your life will you have the dedicated time and freedom to immerse yourself in things that interest you or things that bore you and learn the difference between the two.

Take it from me, after spending over a decade in a career that wasn't a great fit for me, it's easy to see classes as a means to an end, (graduate and get on with my *real* life!) and try to cram your schedule with mandatory classes while skipping electives. But college is *the* time to take some "I wonder" classes: *I wonder what architecture is all about. I wonder if I would like journalism. I wonder if I would be any good at archery.* It may mean it takes you an extra semester to graduate, but you'll be a much more interesting person when you do, and you'll be in a better position to tell the difference between a good job and a job that's good for *you*.

TRAVEL AND DO ALL THE THINGS YOU WANT TO DO BEFORE YOU start a family (that is, *if* you want to start a family).

I know you think that the only reason we keep telling you to consider a semester of college abroad is because your dad and I want fun places to visit, which is true, but the world is a big, wonderful place and there's so much to learn from other cultures. Travel builds your sense of empathy and respect for others, especially when you visit a place where you feel like the "other" for once. And yes, you can certainly still do this after you have a family, but remember how we used to have to feed your brother an entire box of Ritz crackers to make him sit still on the plane? You don't have to do that if you're flying alone.

Always pay with cash or check, and only use credits cards to buy airplane tickets.

Okay, this one made more sense back in the '80s, when people actually knew what checkbooks were, and you didn't face the angry glares of a long line of grocery shoppers if you had the audacity to whip out a checkbook at the register. But the rationale behind it is still sound: Only buy things you can pay for *now*. That being said, even with a tight budget, grandma knew that travel was a good investment, especially travel to visit and build memories with long-distance family and friends.

Date lots of different boys.

This advice was always perplexing to me because Grandma started throwing it at me way before I was allowed to date boys. Plus, even at 13 years old, I knew that this advice had the potential to earn me a pretty nasty reputation at school, so I revised it a bit to "be *friends* with a lot of different boys." Learning to relate to boys in ways that have nothing to do with dating or a physical relationship is a real gift—many of my best friendships were with boys. This was especially easy for me because I had a mullet, Coke-bottle glasses, and headgear – so being friends was a much more realistic goal than dating anyway.

There are lots of fish in the sea.

This one is for when you do start dating and some cute boy breaks your heart. Not only are there a lot of fish in the sea, there are also lakes and rivers all over the country and all over the world. Your heart will be broken by a lot of fish-sticks and farm-raised tilapia, but you deserve Copper River salmon. Sure, they may be harder to come by, but they are worth the wait. Except, since you're a vegetarian, hmmm...There are a lot of carrots in the field.

FISH IN THE SEA, PART B: NEVER CHASE DOWN A BOY OR BEG him to be with you.

Okay, Grandma didn't tell me this one, Oprah Winfrey did (and don't you dare ask, "Who is Oprah Winfrey?"). She once shared a story of some fool who treated her horribly, but as he drove away, she practically jumped on the hood of his car so that he wouldn't leave her. No, I've never literally jumped on a car, but I have metaphorically jumped on some cars by changing the ways I acted or dressed, or by over-looking a boyfriend being disrespectful when I should have used that as the opportunity to kick him to the curb. Refer back to the "fish in the sea" advice. It's cliché because it's true. Plus, there's only room for one fish on your hook so throw the junk fish back in the pond—he's taking up valuable space.

BE CAREFUL WHAT YOU SAY AND DO—THE ONE PERSON YOU don't want to find out always will. (AKA my first boss's version: Don't do or say anything you wouldn't want the world to see on the front page of the *New York Times*.)

Friends will be jerks, teachers will be annoying, and parents will be soooooo lame, but be very careful what and who you confide in. Back in the '80s it took forever for a jilted friend to humiliate you by passing an embarrassing note you wrote around the school. These days it only takes a screenshot and a tweet to instantly broadcast something you did or said to your entire universe of friends (and strangers.). Will you survive the humiliation? Yes, and it will likely be a hilarious story some-day. But spare yourself the drama in the meantime – only say stuff about people that you would be willing to say to their face, or to have your principal read over the intercom at school.

DON'T TAKE SIDES (UNLESS IT'S *YOUR* SIDE).

There's a 99 percent chance that your friend who is pissed off at her boyfriend who is a "lying, stupid, jerk-face who she never ever wants to see again as long as she lives" will be back to holding hands with him by tomorrow. Do not show your support for her by agreeing with all of her angry insults because when she's back with him tomorrow, *you're* the one she'll be mad at. However, if that same boyfriend's behavior goes beyond "jerk" to "dangerous," that is a side that you should take and share with me or another parent or teacher you trust.

LISTEN TO YOUR GUT AND SPEAK UP FOR YOURSELF.

There will be a million instances in your life when you're going to have to make hard decisions without anyone around to help: whether to accept alcohol or drugs, to do more than just kiss some cute boy, to get in a car with someone who has been drinking, to do more than your share on a group project, or accept a job that doesn't sound like a great fit. If you're questioning and doubting what to do, the answer is usually no, and you shouldn't be afraid to listen to your gut and say it. Don't worry about being rude. Don't worry about hurting feelings. Don't worry about needing to come up with an excuse. "No" can be a full sentence by itself. You've only got one you to worry about, and she's my favorite "you" in the world.

YOU'RE PERFECT AND BEAUTIFUL AND I WILL ALWAYS LOVE YOU, no matter what.

It did not take long for me to discover that Grandma was lying when she told me that "*everybody has those little bumps on their arms, you just can't see them.*" (They're keratosis pilaris, by the way, and no, not everybody has them.) However, I think her bigger point was that everybody has something about themselves that they think isn't perfect, but it's all of our combined imperfections that make us who we are. Who you are is amazing and there will never, ever be another one of you in the world. That makes you the most perfect you that there is.

The "no matter what" part usually came up when I was crying in Grandma's arms after getting in trouble for doing something stupid, oh, like the time I went and bought a (mint-condition, cherry-red

Honda Elite Deluxe with digital readout) motor scooter without permission while she was at work and drove it 20 miles home with no helmet on.

Which brings me to the most important, universal parenting rule:

DO AS I SAY, NOT AS I DO. (BETTER YET—DO AS GRANDMA says.)

SUSANNE KERNS IS A WRITER LIVING IN AUSTIN, TEXAS, WITH HER husband and two children. She's currently writing her first book, which she'll finish as soon as her kids stop asking her to "come look at this." Her stories have been featured in several parenting anthologies as well as a variety of websites, including her blogs, SusanneKerns.com and The DustyParachute.com. Susanne was also the co-producer of the 2017 Listen to Your Mother show in Austin. Follow her on Facebook to see why she's frequently featured on Today Parents' "Funniest Parents on Facebook" round-up. You can also find her on Instagram, and sometimes on Twitter when she accidentally hits the wrong button on her phone.

❧ 19 ❧

RUN

BY ALICE GOMSTYN

We need women on the ballot.
We need women on the trail.
We need smart and kind and brazen—brazen!—
Women to prevail.

Calling future heroines and mavens:
We need you to train and run.
We need you to prove the critics wrong,
Who say it can't be done.
We will stand behind you proudly.
We will stomp and chant and cheer.
We will insist, persist, and argue
Until everybody hears:

We need women on the ballot.
We need women on the trail.
We need smart and kind and brazen—brazen!—
Women to prevail.

ALICE GOMSTYN IS A WRITER AND JOURNALIST WHOSE WORK has been published by *The Washington Post*, ABCNews.com, NBCNews.com, Yahoo.com, *Business Insider*, *The Boston Globe*, *The Providence Journal*, and *Babble*, among others. She has also contributed to two parenting humor anthologies. As a senior editor at a content marketing firm, Ms. Gomstyn specializes in business, technology and health articles. When she's not writing and editing, she's promoting important causes as co-founder of the northern New Jersey grassroots group, Glen Rock After the March.

20

EVERYDAY ACTS OF GIRLHOOD REBELLION

BY DANA ARITONOVICH

"A girl should be two things: who and what she wants."

— COCO CHANEL

OHIO, 1980. MY IMMIGRANT GRANDPARENTS' UNFENCED SUBURBAN backyard. I was seven years old and wearing a sensible yet fabulously green ensemble of shorts, a checkered button-down top, and some toe-killers, which was what my family called flip-flops. It was a lovely summer afternoon, a light breeze in the air but the sun approaching scorching hot. I have always loved to marinate in the sun.

Since they lived around the corner, I visited my grandparents often. My middle sister—at this point, my only sister—and I slept over at their house on Fridays and every New Year's Eve. On this day I was visiting *sans* sister, and at this moment I was outside by myself, sitting on the brief concrete patio, my butt resting on an adult-sized lawn chair. I was really living the life that day, taking swigs from a sixteen-ounce glass bottle of Pepsi, emulating the way the men in my family enjoyed their beer.

As sweat began to form on the small of my back, my thoughts turned to watching my father do yardwork topless. I noticed that my mother was never topless in the backyard, and I was curious about it. What was so different about her body? I knew she had boobs, but why couldn't she show them outside like my father showed his? Surely my mom also wanted to keep cool while she worked outside. It didn't make any sense.

In the distant future, I would go out of my way to study the civil rights movement and feminism, always identifying with those who utilized direct action rather than those who preferred patient waiting and assimilation. My first act of public—well, outside my own bedroom walls, anyway—civil disobedience took the shape of unbuttoning my button-down and letting the summer wind flow over my bare skin, Pepsi bottle in hand, feeling completely free and equal in every way. Nobody was around to see my rebellion, but that didn't matter. I chose to live as I pleased, whatever the consequences.

When I was a kid, I always said I wanted to be the one to go out to work so my husband could stay at home and take care of the house and kids and have dinner ready when I got home. My family knew I was serious.

At age seven, I was acutely aware that men and women, boys and girls, were treated differently in the world. My parents had only girls, so my poor father was the only male in our house. It was very clear to me that my mother and father were equals. I never heard my dad speak down to my mom, he didn't call her names or say anything sexist to her. My mother never asked my father permission to do anything (as if!), and she never told him he was right when he was wrong.

Because of my parents, I never internalized what I saw in society that said I had to look and think and feel a certain way because I was a girl. Before I was even five years old, my dad would take me fishing on Saturday mornings; that was our time. I loved getting in the dirt like boys did. I played with toy cars and pretended I was in the Army (thanks to *Stripes* and *Private Benjamin*) and Marines (I salute you, Gomer Pyle!). I pulled the legs off spiders and cut up worms, fascinated that they kept moving for so long. I'd race my yellow plastic Zoomcycle down the driveway into the empty garage, pretending I was doing dangerous, daredevil stunts like Evel Knievel. I taped random wires to my little red wagon, put one of my dad's dirty red rags in my back pocket, and slid myself under that wagon to "fix" it.

My sister and I each had a Barbie townhouse with an elevator in it. We were pretty excited that our Barbies and their families—our main Barbies were first cousins—had such cool, modern homes. They also had sweet Corvettes; mine was a metallic dark blue. We played dress-up with our mom's and grandma's old clothes, competing to see who could create the tackiest outfits; we cleverly called this game Tacky. With two of our human cousins, we pretended we were genies; we even made our own *I Dream of Jeannie* costumes—mine was blue, of course, because I refused to wear anything pink. I have never liked pink, and neither has my mother.

I wasn't told that I shouldn't like what I liked or play how I played. Not by my parents, anyway. Some girls thought they should only like light colors and be polite and quiet and not get themselves dirty. But that was never natural to me. Sometimes I thought I was a bad kid because my grades weren't perfect and I talked too much. I liked being in charge and saying what I wanted to say and standing up to bullies who bothered my sisters. I didn't know how else to be!

When she was a kid, my grandfather taught my mother to do basic plumbing and change a car battery. He wanted her to go to college because he knew that she was really smart and college helped you succeed in America. He encouraged my sisters and me to be competitive, directing us to race each other to the hill at the end of his backyard and back. We were girls and his only grandchildren, and he was so proud. He taught us how to play *tablić*, a popular Serbian card game. He gave us scraps of wood to build things with. He took us around the backyard on the riding mower and let us steer.

We watched our grandmother make soups and special breads for the holidays; sometimes we got to help. She made Serbian doughnuts and crepes for us on the weekends, and always let us drink coffee out of these kitschy plastic green cups with matching saucers. She was a crocheting and knitting phenomenon, and though she was super patient as she tried to teach me, I just never had the knack for it. I was better at making elaborate structures with my Lincoln Logs.

One afternoon we were at a church picnic. My middle sister and I were on the playground with our cousins and kids from Sunday school. In the 1980s, playground equipment wasn't particularly safe. Everything was wood and metal and chain, and though it was sturdy it still broke and had horrible jagged pieces that would definitely give you tetanus.

Two of my cousins were on one end of the ancient, wooden seesaw and I was on the other. Every 30 seconds, they thought it was hilarious to stop so I was stuck up in the air. I was never fond of being practically airborne, so about the fifth time it happened I jumped ship. As I fell the approximately five feet down onto the dirt, my right arm decided to grab a long, sharp splinter sticking out of the seesaw. That daring escape left me with a pretty cool wound that was sure to provide a gruesome scar I could brag about to the kids at school on Monday. My sister ran to tell our mom, who then stomped over to see if I was okay. I didn't cry or complain that it hurt, but I'm sure I blamed my cousins because I've always been a tattletale. After my near-disfiguring injury was cleaned and bandaged, I resumed my regularly scheduled program with the other kids. Nevertheless, I persisted.

In Sunday school as we lined up to go to church, the boys went first because of "tradition." I always heard "ladies first" was how we do it in America, but that certainly wasn't the Serbian way. I was conflicted.

I was at my friend Rori's house during summer break. We were nine years old. Her backyard was pretty big—not really bigger than mine, but it bordered the woods so it seemed bigger. One of her boy neighbors was playing with us. I had met him before, and he was kind of a jerk, actually. He asked me about the music I liked, and when I mentioned The Beach Boys, he laughed. I was annoyed.

"They're old!" he declared. "You listen to that stuff?" This was a dumb question, because obviously The Beach Boys were awesome and I only listened to awesome music.

I explained to him how important The Beach Boys were to the history of rock and roll, how they were influenced by Chuck Berry, and how they made surf music popular. Despite my expertise, he was not swayed. He was even lamer than I thought.

The Beach Boys have been in heavy rotation on my record player since my parents bought me my first one when I turned five and The Beach Boys' music turned seventeen. I listened to my mom's old records all the time, so The Beach Boys, Elvis, Chuck Berry, The Beatles, and Jerry Lee Lewis didn't seem old to me. I produced a radio show on WDRS 113.2 FM in our basement and played their songs for my audience, which consisted of my two sisters (one of whom was a toddler) sitting in the next room.

None of my friends were really interested in this kind of music. Michael Jackson was just about to release *Thriller*—and I was about to become a superfan—but I was still just listening to my parents' music at the time. Whenever I was at Rori's house and that stupid boy was over, he would make fun of me for listening to The Beach Boys. But that didn't matter, because I knew I had good taste in music and could talk to grownups about it and he couldn't.

I took pride in learning about things my schoolmates didn't care about. I obsessively studied everything that interested me: rock and roll, archaeology, stamp collecting, dentistry, Shakespeare. Being an authority was important. If I was ever questioned by some kid who was trying to be a smartass, I wanted to be able to shut them down with my mad knowledge right away.

My parents used to tell me I was strong enough to beat up all the boys. I took that as a compliment. They knew that too many males were intimidated by strong females, and that I wouldn't put up with anyone's crap.

BOYS LOVED MY FRIEND LESLIE. SOME OF THEM SEEMED TO LIKE ME as a friend, but none of them wanted to be my boyfriend in fourth grade. One time I asked Leslie if she could teach me how to get boys to like me, since I really liked boys and wanted to go with somebody already. Her first piece of advice was that I should wear a skirt at least once a week like she did, because all I ever wore were jeans. *Girls who wear pants never get a second glance.*

I was not excited about this suggestion. Skirts and dresses were definitely not my thing, but I still had to wear them to church and weddings and other fancy places. Wearing that stuff to school seemed like a bad idea for many reasons, especially on Fridays because they were Flip-Up Days, meaning the boys were expected to flip up your skirt whenever they could so everyone would see your underwear and laugh at you. Having my personal space violated like that didn't interest me, and I was ready to fight anybody who tried it.

Leslie and I agreed to wear skirts this one day. It was February, but I forced myself to deal with the frigid temperature so I could learn this first of the many important boy-catching secrets Leslie had to share. My mom knew I hated skirts and suspiciously asked why I was dressed like that for school, especially when it was so cold. I told her that I just felt like wearing one that day, and there's no way she believed me.

Ready to fiercely conquer all the ten-year-old boys, I showed up to school in my cute-but-uncomfortable skirt and watched Leslie walk down the hallway. She was wearing pants! I felt betrayed. I asked her right away why she wasn't wearing a skirt since it was her idea that we both do it that day, and she claimed she forgot. I knew she was lying and probably did it because she wanted to make fun of me for being so desperate for attention from the boys. I spent the whole day feeling mad and awkward and freezing in that skirt, just waiting for some stupid boy to try me. And wearing a skirt didn't make even one of them like me.

The next time I decided to wear something other than jeans to school was in warmer weather a year or two later, and I wore it because I felt like it, not because I wanted anyone's attention. It was a button-up denim dress, much more my style since jeans were my life. I still had to be on alert for Friday Flip-Up Day, but was otherwise satisfied with my choice of outfit. In seventh grade, I cut off half that dress and turned it into a denim jacket. That was even better! I drew a big peace symbol on the back of it and put some cool pins on the front. I made myself a set of groovy love beads and wore them to school most days. *Yes*, I told myself, *this is my look now: a hippy born thirty years too late.* Other kids called me a hippy as an insult and constantly asked what I was protesting, but I didn't care. I knew who I was and their opinions didn't affect me.

⟐

WHEN I REALIZED THAT ALL I EVER NEEDED TO DO IN LIFE WAS BE myself, that made everything so much better—not always easier, but I was much happier. I don't apologize for who I am, because who else can I be?

DANA ARITONOVICH GOT OVER HER HATRED OF DRESSES AS A grownup, until she hit 40 and started living in yoga pants. She wore assorted yoga pants while writing essays for Red State Blues: Stories from Midwestern Life on the Left *(2018) and* A Race Anthology: Dispatches and Artifacts from a Segregated City *(2016). Since 2009, Dana has run several blogs including* What I Like Is Sounds *and* Food is the New Sex.

21

SPIRAL PERMS AND OTHER GIANT PILES OF STIFF REGRET

BY KIM FORDE

Spiral perms. They were a thing—a very big thing, literally and figuratively—in New Jersey in the '80s. Bigger. Higher. Taller. Fuller. Pair that chemically altered hair with a can of Aqua Net and a comb, and the sky really was the limit. I have the eleventh-grade school photos to prove it. My girlfriends and I spent considerable time and money on this look, and it required dedication. I can remember getting up for high school before dawn and listening to my favorite cassettes and CDs while I undertook the daily task of readying my hair. My mom tried to tell me, sometimes more subtly than others, that perhaps there would be a day when I looked back on this style with, well, some pause.

What the hell did she know, my 16-year-old self wondered, exasperated by the mere suggestion with my signature audible eye roll.

Turns out she knew a lot. That hair forever remains a giant pile of stiff regret, and also an inescapable time capsule fixture of humiliation in my family.

There's probably some decent analysis out there somewhere about why so many of us teenage girls felt this was a good look, and why we went to such lengths to achieve it. Were we hiding under a shield in those fragile years? Or perhaps we were dressing a part to protect ourselves from the social pitfalls of the high school hallways?

Or—and I'm just spit-balling here—maybe we were just raised in New Jersey in the '80s and we really thought we looked good, as we became self-fulfilling stereotypes that could have put us on a long-term style trajectory with a *Real Housewives* franchise.

That awful and voluminous perm was definitely the most outward sign of what I regretted in my high school years. It's the easiest thing to point to and wish I'd done differently. And, yes, if given the chance, I'd march right into the Department of Life Moment Do-Overs and file a priority application immediately, while frantically waving my 1989 photos. But there were so many other things about those years— choices that shaped who I am—that I'd love another shot at. Because at some point along the way, those years defined me in some binary terms and conditions to which I never should have subscribed, or at least not without some fine print caveats and the representation of a Debate Club captain.

OH, YOU'RE A WRITER. YOU'RE NOT GOOD AT MATH.

GODDAMMIT. TAKE ME BACK TO MRS. DEBLOCK'S ALGEBRA I CLASS, stat, so I can re-do math. Give me all of the math, so I can ignore the ongoing suggestion by teachers and guidance counselors that, because I had a knack for writing, I had found my strong suit—I couldn't also excel at math, and that was okay. You know what? The repeated power of that suggestion had a big impact on me well beyond high school. It guided how little I rounded out my liberal arts classes in college in order to avoid Probability and Statistics. It led me to a corporate life-time of hating workplace finance meetings, thinking I couldn't absorb the nuances, or even have a qualified seat at that table. Because I was the writer girl, not the math girl. It creeps back into my life even now, as I supervise my kids' homework.

Take me back and show me that I'm not committing right here and now to decades of assuming I'm just not good at this. Believe in me the way that the English Department did, by throwing more at me, pushing me, and making me slug through *The Heart is a Lonely Hunter* (the literal worst), *The Odyssey,* and *Ulysses* (alternate title: *Just Kill Me Now, Please, With Irish Whiskey*), even when I thought it was tough and unnecessary. Tell me I will use math in my career because I am going to be accomplished and well-rounded.

YOU'RE THE FUNNY FRIEND. NOT THE PRETTY FRIEND.

YEAH, IT TURNS OUT THAT WISE-ASS GIRLS WITH A BRAIN MAKE many teenage boys highly uncomfortable. But still, no, you don't get to paint me as The Funny One and not One Of The Pretty Ones just because I am quick-witted. Fun fact: I was both, and shame on me for not knowing it at the time (despite my gravity-defying perm, prominent orthodontia, and acid-washed jeans). Why? Because I was parsed into this role of the sarcastic one who didn't put up with a lot of crap from boys drooling their chewing tobacco into bottles while surrounded by giggling, agreeable girls.

One of my most refined talents from a young age was the accuracy of my bullshit meter, having come from a long genetic line of similarly skeptical people. And although a cherished trait, it did land me oftentimes on the social periphery. I took this Funny/Call It As I See It, But Not One Of The Pretty Ones identity with me to college and possibly beyond, dragged it around and leaned on it far more than I should have. How ridiculous. Where were the Tina Feys and the Amy Poehlers then to show me that the Funny Girls can be so much more? If only my 1989 self could see that funny and snarky were not disqualifiers for being attractive, successful fucking badasses. I know this now, but it's less impactful once you reach an age when you start applying eye cream with a firming solution before bed.

I'M NOT BLAMING ANYONE ELSE FOR THESE 1980S DYNAMICS—THIS IS the way things were (if I end this sentence with "back then," please just meet me at Bingo at three in the afternoon, followed by an early buffet dinner). Maybe the perm chemicals seeped into my brain and clouded my judgment, because Lord knows the tanning beds didn't turn out to be harmless. And if I'm being honest, the hair wasn't the only style problem back then. There were also big, elaborate accessories, multiple popped collars, neon, ruffles, and so much more. Even the music—it was loud and offensive and synthetic. It was all so big, so excessive. So assaulting on the senses. And underneath all of it, so much was happening. (Why on Earth did I not major in psychology? Oh, wait, probably because of the math pre-requisites.)

As the height of my hair has settled and even outright flatlined at times over the years, one consistent habit I've had since high school is that my worries, ideas and most plans come about in the dead of night. After I'd untease my 1989 hair and remove my make up, I'd play my cassettes and CDs for hours into the night, wishing I'd understood the math homework and instead writing short stories to fill my brain and my journal, because they came easily. It was then when I wired my life-long body clock to stay up far too late in the quiet to simultaneously accomplish things and worry about every issue over which I have no control (the latter being my specialty). Now, some 30 years later, that has not changed. The things I accomplish and the stories I write and the worries I count have all evolved over time, but their space to breathe and flourish still exist well past an acceptable bedtime. It is a distinct part of who I am and how I operate.

At 16, I worried about math and boys and fashion and being with the right friends, and at 46 I worry about parenting, about my kids being with the right friends and everything else that affects them.

My daughter is nine years old. She is a go-getter who will try anything, anticipate what's next and report back on the nuances of any given situation. Her heart swells with kindness and generosity. Her sense of adventure is boundless, and she does not miss a single thing. Late at night, when I worry and plan and think, I hope she will grow up to surround herself with girls and other influences that won't chip away at her fabulousness, but I wonder how realistic that is.

I want the world for her—all of it, because she will grab it and harness the hell out of it, if given the chance.

If she's not told she has to make choices between things at which she can excel.

If she's not told she can be some things but not others.

She has to know that she can be an All of the Above answer—plus the bonus essay.

KIM FORDE WRITES ABOUT THE ART OF DOMESTIC FAILURE ON HER blog, The Fordeville Diaries. She has appeared in the NYC production of "Listen to Your Mother," and has written for The Huffington Post *and* Scary Mommy. *She was twice named a Humor Voice of the Year by BlogHer and, against all odds of writing full sentences when her three kids are home, this is her seventh humor anthology. When not busy managing her Starbucks addiction and healthy fear of craft stores, she can often be found carbon dating items discovered in the depths of her minivan. She may also spend more time on social media than she is prepared to admit.*

Joy Hedding (signature)

❧ 22 ❧

WHAT IF YOU FLY?

BY JOY HEDDING

What if you fly? I look down at my wrist and see my bracelet. I'm about to take my first certification exam as a snowboard instructor. My classmates are 15, 17, 19, and 31.

I'm 42 years old and have been snowboarding for considerably less time any of these other riders. All have been riding for more than a decade. I'm in year five and this is my first year teaching on the snow. I'm sweating. A lot. "Fearless" reads my other bracelet. "Never Give Up" is on my watch band.

As I take off my bracelets and watch—wristguards, yo!—I repeat each in my head. Over and over.

I get my teaching task for the exam. To pass we must teach an assigned task to our classmates while being observed by the clinic director. We have to instruct in a particular manner and nail the teaching methods. I almost throw up. "Boxes." I have to teach boxes. Boxes are terrain park features a rider or skier can glide across, jump onto, end tap, or slide perpendicular across. In my case, I've ridden many a box on my bum. I'm fearful of falling face first onto a box and have avoided them like the plague since a bad wipe out two seasons ago. On a snowboard, boxes are not a thing I love.

What if you Fly? Fearless. Never Give Up. What if you Fly? Fearless. Never Give Up. What if you Fly? Fearless. Never Give Up. What if you Fly? Fearless. Never Give Up.

You know what? I nailed it. I did it. I did fly. I passed, got my pin, and more inspiration. Now I'm going after my Level 2 certification. In the past few years something has changed. I've changed. No longer do I let fear stop me. I go after what I want. My resume is long, curvy, and disjointed. Software developer, house cleaner, writer, weapon systems instructor, mathematician, mom... all of these things make up me. But not a single one defines me. I'm a moving target for definition. I define me. I want my children to see that a degree doesn't have to dictate who you are. It can be a part of who you are and lead you to any path you choose. It took me until March of 2018 to find my passion. My real and true passion. I wouldn't have found what lights my fire without the long and often circuitous path I've traveled. Remove any of my past experiences and I may still be on the search.

I've been up and down. I've loved jobs and hated them. Sometimes at the same time. But I pushed through. I knew my happy was out there. There have been months, years even, when things simply didn't make sense. I had these little people watching me get through my days. I noticed they emulated things I did. Little things. I drink water with no ice. Three of my four do this. I loved a cold can of soda first thing in the morning. One of them started to try to do this and I quickly gave up soda and switched to coffee. (They never have picked up the making your bed as soon as you wake thing though – it's still something on their chore list.) I am not capable of sitting and 'just' watching television. I have to keep my hands busy—folding laundry, making dinner, stretching—doing something other than just sitting. Watching my children fidget as I do has taught me to seek my calm and if that means cuddles or counting to ten while I make my mind and body quiet, I do it. I want them to be able to be in the moment.

If my kids were emulating the little things, what else were they picking up on? I decided I didn't want them to see me simply 'getting through' my days. I wanted my children to see me embracing life, going after dreams, picking myself up after a fall, and figuring out what to do after a success. Sometimes succeeding is as difficult as failing. Then it's time for the next step. That step can be terrifying.

My oldest is off to college in a few weeks. His path has yet to reveal itself. We had an argument where he succinctly nailed the issue I was having. "I'm adulting. Just not the way you want me to. I'm making decisions and dealing with stuff. In. My. Way."

What if you fly?

What if he flies? Isn't that how we raised him? We get these children for a few short years if we're lucky. We teach them to be independent, self-sufficient humans that we set loose on this planet. He's simply doing what we've prepared him to do his entire life. What if he flies? My girls are still home for years yet. I need to remind myself to be fearless. I don't even own makeup. My 12-year-old ("nearly 13" I hear as she reads over my shoulder) helps me pick out clothing. My 15-year-old keeps me in on what slang terms to use and which are "so last year." My little 10-year-old is so tech-savvy she figured out how to call me on the computer (I had password protected) when our phone lines were down.

My oldest daughter is in the throes of high school. Learning to drive, navigating changing relationships, trying to care for her friends, and already—ALREADY—forgetting that she, too, needs care. I strive to make her understand that taking care of herself is not being selfish. If I can instill in her the drive, the fearlessness to go after her dreams —whatever they may be—I will have done part of my job. She's already on her way, carving a beautiful path. Her journey already has twists and turns, even a few circles, but it belongs to *her*. We talk frequently about the future and yet I remind her to enjoy *today*. Live in the moment so you don't lose today's happy wishing for tomorrow. We are forging that relationship that one day will be a deep friendship. She's a pretty amazing human.

My littles. They aren't so little anymore. Each is nearly as tall as me. Although we all look alike in some ways, we are drastically different. Physically, emotionally, and personality-wise. Feisty in their unique ways, they will own their worlds. One is ready to take on each day, balls the wall, bull by the horns, and full of more energy than a classroom of kindies. Her happiness is infectious and even when she's down, she'll flash that megawatt smile, giggle, and find her path back to happy. She's my mini-me and while I see epic battles in our future, I also see the beginnings of the closeness we will share.

The other greets the day in her quiet, calm, self-assured manner. She observes and puts a plan into action that others simply follow. This one a natural leader although I don't think she yet realizes it. She doesn't say as much as the others, yet the words she chooses to share create a spark in those around her. I never want her to lose herself in the ever changing landscape of middle school and the challenges she will encounter. As she gains confidence, she will soar. One day she and I will be confidants.

How? How did I get so lucky?

Teaching each of these children to fly while learning myself has been a challenge. If you've ever flown, the crew always reminds you to put on your mask before assisting others if there's an emergency. I needed to take time, teach myself to fly and be fearless, before I could teach them. And they watched. They saw me take a beating during falls on my snowboard, get rejection after rejection writing, dismiss toxic friends, and stagger through challenging work days. I got up each time. Sometimes more slowly than others, but I always got up. They also watched as I chased after and caught a few of my dreams. At times I feel guilty for leaving them for an extra week in the winter to be in the mountains. Then I remember. I remember I'm taking care of me, setting a good example, and will come home refreshed. My cup will be full and I'll be ready to face another day—whatever that day may be.

My kids see me navigating life a with a smile. Because life is too short to not get after it. Go for it. If you don't ask, if you don't try, if you don't seek... let's flip that around. Why not ask? Why not try? Why not seek? If my children try, I consider what they did a success. Sometimes that first step is the hardest and taking it needs to be celebrated. Played a ball game that didn't go well? Did you have fun? WINNER WINNER CHICKEN DINNER. Tried a new trick on the snowboard and ate snow? Are you ready to go again? Yes? GAME ON. Life is about seeking your happy. And enjoying the path to find it.

If you're always waiting on the next step, you're wasting what's right in front of you. If you're not happy, change your path. Be empowered. You don't have to be stuck. Take the challenge of where you are right now, map a route forward towards what you want and take that first step. No. *Leap* for that first step. You can do it. If you find that path has led you to the wrong location, try, try again. Keep on trying because *what if you fly?*

My happy is out there waiting for me. I've got to go now. It's time to take another step. My kids are watching.

JOY HEDDING IS A SNOWBOARDING FANATIC AND LOVES TO SHARE her exploits – snowboarding and otherwise – on Instagram. Frequently funny, always honest, and occasionally serious, Joy blogs about everything from dealing with teenagers to navigating life after PTSD. Joy has been published in Surviving Mental Illness Through Humor *and* Only Trollops Shave Above the Knee *and been featured on RealityMoms.rocks and UrbanMommies.com. Her blog is Evil Joy Speaks and you can find her on Facebook, Twitter, Instagram, and Pinterest.*

✣ 23 ✣

BETTER THAN A BOYFRIEND

BY DORRIT CORWIN

The summer of 2013 was my second of five summers spent at all girls sleep-away camp in rural New Hampshire. I was ecstatic to be back with the friends I had made the year before in an environment that fosters creativity, collaboration, and personal growth. To this day, there is no place where I feel as safe and as genuine as I do at camp.

Upon my arrival, I was greeted by familiar smiles from far and wide, as well as many new faces. By the end of day one, I knew almost everyone in my bunk by name, except for one girl who hadn't said a single word to anyone. She sat in the corner with her rainbow loom, vigorously folding rubber bands over plastic pegs to create bracelets that symbolize friendship, though she didn't yet have any friends, herself.

I asked if she would make me one—not because I thought she was cool and wanted to actually be her friend, but because her bracelets were cool and I wanted to wear one. At twelve years old I was already fixated on my relationships and how others perceived them. A necessary break from our fabricated Instagram lives for a month meant popularity was determined by how much skin was showing between

SEVERAL SASSY SCRIBES

your wrist and your elbow. The more friendship bracelets you wore, the more friends you had.

The girl finished my bracelet later that evening. She tightened it around my wrist and looked at me through doughy aqua eyes. "I'm Sophie," she said, "I'm from Connecticut." She already knew exactly who I was and where I was from because I was so excited to be back at camp that I hadn't shut up all day. I was fairly certain she thought I was insane and that she had absolutely no interest in the bracelet she made me acquiring any kind of deeper meaning of friendship. "It's nice to meet you!" I said, "You're really good at making bracelets."

It wasn't a "and the rest was history" moment, but it was certainly a start. Due to the close proximity of everyone during camp, bonds build quickly. Each day that passes feels like a week, and each week feels like a month. On our walks to and from the waterfront, Sophie and I talked music, politics, and family life. By our third or fourth trip back from water skiing, Sophie was so captivated by the stories I had told her about my grandmother that she decided to write her a letter. Soon, they were exchanging notes weekly, and my grandma was booking a plane ticket for Sophie to come meet her the following February.

It was like talking to a mirror. Sophie and I would sit on my top bunk during rest hour, my iPod on shuffle, flipping through home magazines and designing our very own beach house. I'd skip a song with the assumption that no one but me would actually listen to it, and Sophie would ask me to go back because she knew by the sound of the first three cords that it was one of her favorites.

It didn't take long for us to become recognized as a dynamic duo of sorts. We harassed the camp photographer to take photos of us for our parents. We showered together (in side by side showers), brushed our teeth together, and stayed up late together, ranting about our disappointment in certain bunkmates' limited knowledge of current events and the American government. Together we neglected to complete our chores, took ourselves on impromptu adventures, and made our counselors' jobs extremely difficult. Yet, some of these counselors have remained our dearest friends and supporters as they have watched our relationship grow and blossom into something incredibly special.

Over the next three summers and two years, Sophie and I would grow so close that by our final summer at camp, we'd shed a tear not out of the fear of never seeing each other again but because we both knew that the second we crossed the border into Massachusetts, we were losing a vital part of our childhoods. We'd never again be enveloped by greenery and surrounded by our best friends without the distraction of technology. Every time I'd see her after our final camp-fire, my iPhone would be in my back pocket. It wouldn't necessarily be a bad thing, but it would never be the same.

Two years have passed since our final campfire, but our friend-ship has only grown stronger in each other's absence. I talk to Sophie every day – multiple times per day. Since she is always three hours ahead of me, she wakes up to texts that contain random thoughts I have between 9 p.m. Western Time and 6 a.m. Eastern Time, and I wake up to a good morning text from her. We send each other memes, sometimes the same ones without even meaning to. We pick out each other's outfits. We wish each other good luck on every test we take. We know each other's weekend plans. We wish each other's parents happy birthdays and happy anniversaries. We track each other's locations, and when the blue dots on the map meet together, it's like the stars have aligned.

Even our friends at home know that while our bonds with them might be strong, the bond we have with each other is on a completely different level. When I went to visit Sophie in Westport this September, she took me to a party at her friend's house. As I walked downstairs into the furnished basement, a setting I don't normally encounter in Los Angeles, everyone stopped what they were doing and sprinted in my direction. "Dorrit!" they shouted in unison, "We have heard SO much about you!" Since this was true, it was like I'd known them all for years.

The same has been true when Sophie has visited me. She crashed my Thanksgiving dinner this year, and it was as if I simply gained a twin at the table. My parents treat her like their fourth child and my grandparents like their sixth grandchild. We are so frighteningly similar that we've had the exact same feelings towards every college we've each visited on separate occasions, so her mom eventually figured that rather than waste time and money touring a bunch of schools, they'd just use my list!

Sophie is the only friend I've ever had who I've never had a legitimate fight with. We never argue, and we never disagree because we are simply the same exact person. It's not like the cliché of a best friend who is more of a sister because I fight with my sister all the time about trivial matters. Sophie falls somewhere between a best friend and a lover—like a boyfriend, but better.

Whenever we're together, our lives miraculously seem to change for the better. The weekend adventures we've planned to New York City and Boston have worked out so seamlessly that being with her truly feels like a dream. We've decided that since we are quite literally each other's lucky charm, we'll be living together after college in an apartment in New York City. We'll both hit our strides at the exact same time because living together will be the ultimate dream. We'll be each other's maids of honor, have our kids at the same time, raise them together, and vacation together... Our husbands will be there, too, I guess.

Most teenage girls fantasize about weddings, college, and tropical vacations, but I fantasize about my truly wonderful and irreplaceable best friend. It's almost like we're dating. People have asked me if we are. And honestly, if we weren't straight, we would make the long distance relationship thing work and be everyone's favorite power couple.

Yes, the friendships I made and life skills I learned at camp changed my life. But the five summers I spent at camp were the only time periods during which I had no access to my phone and the Internet, which is something I took entirely for granted. Since my final summer in 2016 when I went without my phone for a month, the longest I've spent without it is a few hours. And I hate it.

Yet at the same time, my friendship with Sophie would most likely not still exist if it weren't for technology and social media. While my relationship with my phone might be love/hate, my relationship with Sophie is absolutely nothing but love. I am so blessed to be her best friend, and I cannot imagine my adolescence without her as my rock, keeping me grounded and loved from 3,500 miles away.

DORRIT CORWIN, A SENIOR AT MARLBOROUGH SCHOOL IN LOS Angeles, serves as editor in chief of the art and literature magazine and writes a music column for the school newspaper. "Peaches & Mangoes," a short story she wrote at the Kenyon Review Young Writers' Workshop, won a Scholastic Gold Key and was published in Smith College's Voices and Visions Journal. The Rising Voices Fellowship combined Dorrit's passions for writing, Judaism, feminism, and social justice, and she serves on the Teen Editorial Board for Fresh Ink for Teens.

❦ 24 ❦

GO-GO GIRL

BY JENN BELDEN

When I was in seventh grade, I was a very awkward 12-year-old. It was the early '80s, when perms were all the rage, and my mother who disliked her straight, limp hair also despaired of *my* straight, limp hair, so off to the beauty salon she dragged me to rectify the situation with smelly chemical wave solution and colorful plastic curlers and mortification.

As the mentality at that time was a tight curl would last longer than a loose curl, a tight curly perm it was. I was more Jan Brady (with the bad wig) awkward than Marsha, sleek and popular. Combine that with glasses, horsey braced teeth, and hand-me-downs from an older cousin with a penchant for buying a shirt or pair of chinos in *all* the colors if she liked the style, and I was a sight to behold. Stir in a bucket of self-consciousness and a cup or two of self-criticism, and mix with a complete lack of athleticism and a massive love of books, and you have the hot mess that was me.

I was (as I still am) very introverted except when around my closest friends. It was helpful that both my seventh and eighth grade classes were composed of 14 people—seven boys and seven girls. Helpful, that is, until someone decided *you* would be the center of negative attention (for whatever reason they came up with).

Then as now, standing out was not a goal. Attention is one thing; it's safe to say most people enjoy positive attention, but being the *center* of attention created dread in the pit of my stomach.

Enter the period of the Go-Go Girl.

Thinking about it all these years later, I still cringe.

It was an ordinary day when I walked onto the playground for lunch recess, only to be greeted by the shout of "Hey, Go-Go Girl!" It took a few more shouts and laughs to realize the hoots and calls were directed at me.

Go-Go Girl? Being 12 or so, I possessed a vague idea of what a go-go dancer was, and believe me, that description couldn't be further from reality. We're talking about a plain schoolgirl in a Catholic elementary, complete with nuns, planted in a small town in the Midwest—and far from any dance club, with the closest thing to spur even the image of go-go boots being the *Soul Train* reruns after school. My dependable footwear at that age was either polished penny loafers (complete with a shiny penny in the little pocket), no-name deck shoes, or inexpensive tennis shoes purchased at Value City, and the closest thing to risqué might have been my purloined, forbidden copy of Judy Blume's *Are You There God? It's Me, Margaret.*

Soon, more boys in the seventh and eighth grades caught on and joined in to the catcalls when I entered a classroom or the cafeteria, or even during PE class when I was up for bat, or knocked out in the hated dodgeball matches. They may as well have been lobbing rotten tomatoes at my head for how mortifying it felt. In reality, it likely lasted only a few weeks, but it felt like forever and the humiliation was complete. I felt one step away from getting a bucket of pig blood dumped on me at prom, only without Carrie's supernatural ability and a really uninspired, dorky nickname.

It shouldn't have hurt so badly, hearing those words, but they cut deep. In hindsight, I think pain and distress from words like that come from the want for understanding. It's just a three-letter, one word question, "Why?" but it takes on gargantuan weight when seeking reason. If you're thin-skinned, it's simply excruciating.

Hindsight and experience revealed that there was likely no reason for it other than one (a) obnoxious or (b) equally awkward and trying-to-fit-in pre-pubescent boy overheard the phrase somewhere and decided it was as good a time as any to use it. Some adults even offered the suggestion that one of the boys might have had a crush on me, to which I responded in horror: "Why would they think that would make me LIKE them?"

It wasn't the first time that a stupid phrase lobbed my way utterly stopped me in my tracks. In high school, it was members of the football team who would hoot the nickname of the boy I was dating any time I walked into the cafeteria. (I broke up with him because it was easier than sinking into the metal folding chairs.) It happened later, in college, when the instructor of my two-dimensional design class mocked me with taunts of "middle class and mediocre"—because in his world, middle-class kids didn't suffer and one needed to suffer to create good art, and absolutely nothing I did met with his approval. At the end of the semester, I ended up changing my major instead of enduring the other requisite design courses he taught, my confidence crushed.

That I could allow the words of another to cut so easily baffled and frustrated me. My skin was tanned, smooth—and paper thin—and I might have sold my former altar girl soul to make it thicker. I loved words—but the perfect comeback struck later, when I was alone in my room replaying the day's latest mortification in my head.

Years later, I found myself blessed with a fearless, spunky and outgoing little girl. That side of her personality clearly came from her father; from me, she inherited anxiety and imagination.

Lucky kid.

But here's the rub—no matter how confident a face a person puts on, no matter how outgoing they might be, kids can still be hurtful and cruel and words still sting. And here I was, tasked with teaching her how to stand up for herself and not be cowed by the words of others, when I had failed so badly myself.

I would teach my girl to stand up for herself. She would develop her self-worth. She would learn to stand up for herself, and *never* accept "Oh, that's just how he shows you he likes you" as justification for any bad boy behavior. She would demand more.

She would be everything I wasn't, my heart sang as my fist punched the sky.

Which all sounds well and good in theory. It's easy to give advice when you are standing on the outside, but true learning and growth really comes from personal experience, and the ability of kids to be cruel or to box you out from the rest of your group is timeless. So we talk, a lot: about different ways to handle a situation, about when to get an adult involved, about when it's best to stick up for yourself.

We talk about how the best way to defuse a bully is to take away his or her power, which is really both your attention and your fear, and we practice responses because words *are* a weapon if used wisely to protect and not to stab back. Politely but dryly responding, "Wow, that took a lot of thought, thanks for sharing" and sealing it with a big smile before walking away confuses the pants off of most bullies. When a boy is mean to a girl, calling him on it with a surprised, "Is that comment supposed to impress me? It's not working!" takes the steam out of their approach.

She may also have punched a boy when he and his group of friends repeatedly followed her and a friend home from school, taunting and being cruel with words she would not even repeat to me, and refusing to leave them alone. I can't say it is something I would have done myself, but I suppose if you say "Stop, or else," you follow up with the "or else." She stood her ground and they never tried it again.

The biggest lesson to be imparted was the hardest learned by me, and that is that you should never, ever value your worth through the eyes of others. Be true to yourself and hold your head high, because you are wonderfully made; people that try to bring you down to lift themselves up should be pitied, and cut from your life (or pushed to the side until they come to appreciate you and all your bad jokes and quirks.) There's really no avoiding hurt, not if you want to live a full life that is true to yourself, so you allow yourself that cry and then you walk out tall and as confident as you can muster.

Find your people. Surround yourself with people who have your back, and who are just as goofy or awkward or curious or interesting as you are.

My daughter is petite and quirky and mismatched socks and one hundred percent her own person. She feels deeply, for herself and for others, and that makes her an easy target.

But now she can ask herself of the bully *"Would I choose to be friends with them if I were to pick first?"* and realize that the often answer is likely *"no,"* regardless of how popular that person is. She can hear the words thrown at her, and she can take a step back and figure out where they come from. (Is it jealousy? Is it hurt? Is it a badly worded demand for attention?) And she knows that is absolutely okay to cry when her heart or her ego or her confidence is wounded, because that is a perfectly normal response. Crying doesn't make you weak, but when you're done, you have to dry your tears and put on your game face and let them see that they can't beat you down.

And she knows she can throw a clean right hook, thanks to her mixed martial arts classes, although I pray that never becomes necessary. (The boys are a little afraid of her anyway.) Fierce balances well with unicorn tees and iridescent Converse high tops.

She still has the rest of middle school and high school to navigate, but the 12-year-old Go-Go Girl I was admires her and thinks she'll do just fine.

JENN BELDEN IS A WRITER AND MOTHER TO A TEEN, A TWEEN, AND one slightly mad spaniel. She is the voice behind the blog Momma on the Rocks, where she writes to avoid folding laundry or ever finishing her book. Her life goal is to finish a cup of coffee before she loses it somewhere in her house. Jenn's writing been featured on Mamalode and HumorWriters.org. You can find her at mommaontherocks.com and on Twitter @jenncaffeinated.

25

HERE BE DRAGONS . . . AND THEIR CUPCAKES

BY E. R. CATALANO

You could say I went out of my comfort zone when I had my daughter.

First, with the whole pregnancy and childbirth thing. Of course, both of those are probably outside the comfort zone for most women. Unless their zones include nausea and heartburn. And they can chillax while having labor induced which doesn't work and so after 36 hours with no progress they end up having a C-section, which was my experience.

So pregnancy and childbirth were outside of my zone, which, if I'm being honest, is fairly limited. Its borders actually begin and end at my couch, where I like to sit reading a book and drinking chai, an old sweater stretched over my knees.

So why did I do it? Why does anyone do what they're afraid to do? Why did Magellan, who saw the map with "here be dragons" written in the margins, still say, "I'm going to circumnavigate this mofo,"—"circum" being the part of the word on which he'd hung his hopes? Because Magellan wagered the reward was greater than the risk.

I was just like an intrepid sixteenth-century explorer, except I was a twenty-first-century woman who'd reached her late-thirties with not a lot of desire but a lot of fear surrounding having a child yet still thought, "Well, Dwindling Egg Supply, it's now or never." Okay, so maybe Magellan had more ambition.

After pregnancy and childbirth, the child itself will require you to leave your comfort zone. A lot. The discomfort I've experienced since my daughter was born has ranged from physical discomfort—holding a crying sleepless child all night, being vomited on, frequenting unsavory bathrooms due to avoidable "emergencies"—to the emotional discomfort of socializing with strangers at kids' birthday parties, arranging play dates, and realizing you have become your mother.

Love for a child can take you way off the map. I'd also been afraid when I learned I was having a girl that I'd fail her somehow.

I'd long struggled with the question of what it meant to be a woman and if that was the same as being feminine. I've always felt uncomfortable with femininity, both because the rigid roles that went with it rankled me as a feminist—nurturing mother, demure and passive wife or girlfriend—and also because I felt myself a failure at achieving them—I didn't like wearing dresses, hated manicures and pedicures, etc.

Sure, these were clichés, but I was still afraid that if my daughter loved princesses or other girly things, my disapproval might show through and, at best, I'd ruin her fun, and at worst, damage her sense of self. How could I balance being myself with letting her be *herself*, especially if that meant hiding my opinion of what she liked? Turns out all my agonizing was for nothing since children have a way of thwarting our expectations, good and bad.

Here, after all, be dragons.

And by "here" I mean, in my own home.

I'm not being metaphorical. I think my daughter is a dragon. She certainly wishes she was. She LOVES dragons and anything dragon related. We have all the dragon Lego sets, tons of dragon books, toys, and figurines. She draws pictures of dragons. Her name, she told me the other day, is Drago the Destroyer. The next day it was Dragon Girl 19. Why 19? I asked. Because one and nine are her favorite numbers, silly.

Number confusion aside, dragons are way cooler than princesses, so I supported her in her love, bought all the dragon things, oohed and aahed over all the dragon stories she told me. Then came her birthday, for which she wanted a dragon theme, naturally. And here's where my whole "you be you and I'll be me" personal practice turned into "I'll be someone else so my daughter can be a dragon." All because I decided to make Dragon Fire Cupcakes from a recipe I'd seen on Pinterest.

Note: As you can guess from what I previously said regarding all things feminine, I am not a Pinteresty/arts-and-crafty/cake-from-scratchy kind of mom/person. But, god help me, I wanted to make my dragon daughter happy. Magellan faced sea monsters; surely, I could face decorative baking. Plus, you only live once, so you might as well torture yourself to please a seven-year-old who hasn't learned empathy yet.

This would be my first time using a pastry bag to apply icing. Previously I'd only ever used the tried-and-true dull-knife method. *And* I needed to apply three different colors of icing: red, orange, and yellow, the main three colors comprising "dragon fire."

On, now, to the tragic display of humanity that was me loading a pastry bag with three separate colors and trying to keep them separate and then trying to pump them through the icing-delivery-system nozzle thing that was supposed to create swirls of yummy-tasting, amazing-looking, verisimilitudinous dragon fire.

DRAGON FIRE CUPCAKES (AS MADE BY ME)

Step 1: Buy cake mix from the store and make the damn cupcakes.

(I used Devil's Food because that's the alias chocolate uses when it wants to seem "street.")

Step 2: Buy pre-made buttercream frosting, icing-delivery nozzles, pastry bags, food dye in red, orange, and yellow.

Step 3: Go back to store because you mistakenly bought two oranges and zero yellow.

Step 4: Watch online tutorials on how to add color to your buttercream frosting.

Then do that part, after washing your cereal bowl from breakfast because you only had two clean bowls and you'll need three (which later turns out to be four).

Step 5: Watch online tutorials for how to load a pastry bag in general and how to load a pastry bag with three different colors.

Try doing that. Get frosting all over your hands. Clean hands and watch another tutorial. Try again. Same result. Sigh. Press on. Literally. (By the way, do you know how much hand strength it takes to squeeze buttercream frosting through those icing nozzles? I wouldn't want to make a pastry chef angry is all I'm saying. They could probably crush your throat with one hand. While icing your funeral cupcake with the other.)

Step 6: Keep trying, Mother of Dragons!

Try a different nozzle. Try different wrist movements. Visualize the word "finesse."

Scoop frosting off cupcakes and get another bowl and then load that mixed-color frosting into a new pastry bag. Despair of ever getting the three colors to feed evenly. Have a vision of the future in which the pastry bag explodes, shooting frosting everywhere.

Your vision is half right.

The pastry bag does indeed explode, but the frosting shoots out in only one direction, onto your shirt, your dirty, tasty shirt. You probably should've put your antipathy toward feminine clichés aside and worn the apron you'd received as a gift from someone who doesn't know you.

Also, you should've noticed that you'd been losing bag integrity, but you'd been so focused on the icing struggle itself. Varying pressure, placement, and wrist flicks be damned, you cannot make the cupcakes look like they had on Pinterest. Orangey-red schmush is not dragon fire.

Step 7: Remember, perfect is the enemy of good, and decide that perfect cupcakes are as mythical as dragons.

AKA, you're done.

All told, I watched eight damn YouTube tutorials on icing cupcakes. How did they make it look so easy? Why didn't they warn me it was harder than it looked? How did that one lady with perfect makeup ice cupcakes while wearing trumpet sleeves? Trumpet. Sleeves.

Still, one thing I had learned, albeit too late to avoid the day's drama, was to have faith in myself. And by that I mean faith in *my estimation* of myself, and my skills, including where they fall short. As my inner motivational speaker often says, "Liz, you *can't* do this. But, sweetie, that's okay. You're good at reading. And drinking chai. I guess." She is supportive but pragmatic.

So my Dragon Fire Cupcakes were not what I'd hoped, and it took me so long I was unable to finish before my daughter dragon came back from an outing with the Husband.

When she came in, she saw the sugary crime scene, and looked at me like, *Explain.*

I told her I was making Dragon Fire Cupcakes for her birthday and she looked at the cupcakes for a few moments before turning back to me, and patting my frosting-covered hand, she said, "At least you tried. That's what's important."

Empathy, after all.

E. R. CATALANO IS THE MOTHER OF ONE EVIL MASTERMIND LIVING IN *Brooklyn, New York, and writes a humor blog at zoevstheuniverse.com. She is a contributor to* But Did You Die? *and* I Just Want to Be Perfect, *the previous two books in the* Pee Alone *series;* The Bigger Book of Parenting Tweets; *and* Lose the Cape: Never Will I Ever (and Then I Had Kids); *and her humorous essays have appeared on* McSweeney's, RAZED, The Huffington Post, Little Old Lady Comedy, MockMom, *and* Scary Mommy, *among others. Today Parents has also named her one of the "Funniest Parents on Facebook." Though some may say she exaggerates when it comes to the antics of her seven-year-old offspring, her actual fiction can be found online and in literary magazines. She's currently working on a novel about Nancy Drew called* Becoming the Girl Detective *as well as a collection of short stories called* Prove You're Not a Robot. *Please follow her on Twitter at @zoevsuniverse and on Facebook. She needs all the validation she can get!*

26

THIS ONE IS FOR THE GHOST GIRLS

BY KIM BONGIORNO

I was born a ghost girl.

Colorless and silent, I floated into my family and settled in place at the end of the line. It didn't take long for me to understand that my invisibility was a gift.

Our home was pungent with a potpourri of order held in rough dishes of fear that would appear in every room with no notice. The floors were patterned with uncrossable lines drawn years before I arrived, color-coded by gender. I had many more lines I could not step over than my brothers. Girls cooked, baked, set the table. Girls swept, washed, hung the laundry. Girls were to be barely seen and never heard. If they were heard, it was when called upon and only a recording of what they had been told girls were allowed to say or think or report.

When I was little, none of this made me angry. Logic told me it was wrong, but I was too busy learning and following the rules to bother with feelings. Emotions, opinions, and words were things I kept pressed inside in my belly. Those were bright, colorful adornments too risky to release: they'd draw attention. Luckily, I wasn't particularly striking at the time. Beauty and pigment weren't interested in phantoms.

It was exactly as it was supposed to be. I remained, if anyone bothered to glance my way, benign. Men didn't bother hiding their disinterest in my presence. They never asked why I had come.

Eventually, I became old enough to go to school. In a habit of watching and reading people rather than engaging with them, I got to know my classmates and teachers well before they knew me at all. I was the peaceful apparition in the schoolyard, one they became so used to they'd forget it was there. But my name was still on the class list, so sometimes I was invited to social gatherings. I used them to collect more data. One thing was clear: Whether at a home, restaurant, or roller rink, the men were in charge and the boys were in training to be in charge. Not all of them took advantage of their positioning in hurtful ways, but they didn't seem too bothered by having an advantage that hurt the beloved girls and women in their lives. They weren't offering to give it up. Girls craftily achieved power within their gender by means of small cruelties played out by withholding friendship bracelets or sleepovers in front of an audience.

I got older.

I stayed silent.

I kept watching.

Other adults took my silence and restraint as a sign of maturity, and at an age far too young to be in charge of other human beings I was asked to babysit. The family consisted of an exhausted woman in frumpy, ill-fitting clothes and a sharp-dressed husband who barely looked at her unless they were making yet another child to put in my care for far below minimum wage. Over time I understood that the father and sons were of highest importance under that roof, watching the mother turn away time and time again, biting her lip instead of offering a correction, opinion, or need to a disinterested audience. At times when we were alone, she'd get lost in telling me stories over tea. Her light would slip through the cracks, dazzling me, but then her husband would come home wondering why dinner wasn't ready, spackling over what I just witnessed until I questioned whether I ever saw it at all.

I started feeling angry.

I stayed silent.

I kept watching.

It was this babysitting job that earned me the money to treat myself to something I never thought I'd wear: stripes. Slim black and white ones dashed horizontally across a skirt passable for trendy. Thrilled with my purchase and hoping I'd be seen that day at school, I walked into our kitchen to eat breakfast with my head held high. One brief scan of my outfit from his throne at the kitchen table and I wasn't allowed out of the house, for only a whore would wear a skirt like that. Sure, I hadn't yet so much as kissed a boy, but my hemline grazed the top of my kneecap and, really, what was the difference between me and a woman who allowed men to masturbate inside her for cash? Clearly nothing anymore, for this was a truth as declared by the man of the house. I faded from his presence like mist, pulled off the whole outfit, shoved it to the back of my closet, and changed back into something that felt like shadows again.

The skirt debacle piqued my curiosity, so I quietly paid more attention to what people wore, what people thought about what other people wore. The message was clear: I was not the only whore around. Men made the rules and it was so easy for us females to break them: a neckline that dipped, a hem that rode up, a heel higher than on grandma's church shoes and it was determined that the girl was easy. How could she possibly complain about a guy getting handsy if she dressed in a way that showed her appealing curves? She was asking for it.

I got angrier.

I stayed silent.

I kept watching.

Soon I had curves of my own and the hands started reaching for me. Boys in school halls, grown men at the movies, strangers passing me by as I trailed behind my mother during errands—they'd squeeze my butt or brush my breast or try to slide their hand up my thigh without permission, without warning, without even introducing themselves first. I was confused because I followed their dress code. I fought away the hands, but did not tell on them. Who would I tell? The people in power were on the same team as the people I wanted ejected from the game. There was no way they'd do it, that's not how you win.

When I was twelve someone saw me at the mall. As much as I

tried to fade from view, a professional scout recognized that the planes of my face formed angles that the light liked and my bones stretched up, up, up against my preference for shrinking away. It made them see dollar signs. They took a Polaroid and handed me a business card. They kept the Polaroid and I gave my parents the business card. When my father saw dollar signs, too, I suddenly had value. A fluke of genetics gave me value. Not my heart or mind or ability to make my brothers laugh so hard they spewed milk from their noses. It was what it was, and at least it was a safety net instead of a cage. I tolerated being inspected like a cow at auction, judged for what appealed to men over anything else. It wasn't different than any other day, really. I couldn't complain.

I got angrier.

I stayed silent.

I kept watching.

Despite my penchant for hiding behind walls of my own construction, I made a group of female friends. We climbed out of childhood into womanhood together. We forgave one another our missteps. We respected one another's boundaries. We traded lipsticks and laughs. When I was with them I felt safe enough to share my emotions, opinions, and words. I felt like a real person.

My friends began dating, so I dipped my toe in, too. I was hard to catch, often disappearing right when someone was ready to talk. If he stood very still, I'd eventually float his way, appear before him with a smile. But just because a boy genuinely liked me didn't mean he would stop putting his wants first. I backed off. I knew I deserved better than that. I'd try again and have to physically fight a date off of me after saying, "I said no" far too many times. I saw my friends get hurt over and over again, get physical with boys before they wanted to over and over again. Romance shouldn't be so sad. Love shouldn't feel like you've relented. None of it sat well with me.

I got angrier.

I stayed silent.

I kept watching.

It was a typical Thanksgiving dinner. Various male family members sat around the table as the girls and women set food before them, discarded aprons, ensured there was salt and pepper within reach of both ends of the party, as was expected of them. My mother went to grab one last thing as I sat with a straight back, hands on my lap, as was expected of me. Nobody touched their food until the last person sat. That last person was always Mom. As she rattled around in the kitchen—always a servant, never the served—my father made a derogatory joke about "broads," the term he regularly used when referring to women.

In that moment, the anger that had been building in me for years finally pushed me into full form. My flesh flushed pink with rage, my eyes steel with determination. My hands were blotched like bruises in white-knuckled fists, raspberry crescent moons forming on my palms beneath my nails. I was possessed with too much understanding of my failure to be nothing but a bystander and how that only helped the misogyny thrive around me. The disrespect of women had gone on too long. I had a choice to make: Take my anger at the unfairness I had experienced out on others in order to get my own power, or use it to fuel myself to help correct the balance of power for everyone. It was an easy choice. I slammed my fist on the table, silencing the room.

"You are never to use that word to refer to my mother or any other woman again."

I turned and looked him in the eye. "Never."

Everyone froze. My gut told me I would pay for the scene, but I did not care. Let there be witnesses.

I simmered, fists clenched, prepared. He did not get up. He did not yell. He looked at me as if a stranger had taken his youngest child's seat and he was contemplating what to do about it. He chose to tell my sister to pass the turkey. Everyone sprang into motion, flicking napkins onto laps, scooping vegetables onto plates. I slid my arm back under the table, unfurled my hands, and released the breath I had been holding, exhilarated.

The silence I wore for 16 years was peeled off by pure rage. Maybe I couldn't end misogyny altogether, but I had to start trying. My first step was taken while seated, but there was no question that I was moving in a new direction.

From that point on, I stubbornly became part of the solution.

I drew my own uncrossable lines. I stroked the hair of girls who needed to be told their true value. I made eye contact with boys and was clear about how girls are to be treated. I publicly and privately questioned authority. I donated time when I had that and money when I got enough. I continued being angry, watching and listening, picking and choosing when and how I could make a difference. They didn't all have to be big changes. Little ones add up. Hope grows. I did it imperfectly, but I tried. I got better at it over time.

I often thought of the sound of my fist hitting that table, announcing that I was present and to be accounted for.

The ghost girl still lives inside of me, though our form is more that of a vengeful revenant now. Able to hide in plain sight when needed, I relentlessly haunt the patriarchy to take misogynistic men down, strip them of the power they stole from women by force, coercion, or negligence. They think they can run, they think they can hide, but I find them. When I do, I reveal myself. I rattle my chains in their ears. I whisper with a grin, "I came for you."

KIM BONGIORNO IS THE AUTHOR AND FREELANCE WRITER BEHIND the blog Let Me Start By Saying. A crafter of everything from funny parenting tweets to fantastical fiction, her work has received praise from the likes of Buzzfeed, The Today Show, The Huffington Post, *and The Erma Bombeck Writers' Workshop. Kim lives in New Jersey with her family, who are wonderfully tolerant of her book hoarding tendencies. Learn more at kimbongiornowrites.com.*

27

OF STARBUCKS AND SHIN-KICKING—MY FRAUGHT CHILDHOOD ATTEMPTS AT FEMINISM

BY MEGAN SULLIVAN

S ince I was old enough to understand the word, I've proudly called myself a feminist. I just wasn't always very good at it.

Oh, sure, I tried—my heart was in it, but that didn't mean I knew what I was doing. My parents encouraged me to read and play in the mud and do anything a boy could do, which are great lessons unless your kid is a loose cannon with a penchant for starting drama in the good name of Women's Rights.

Case in point: When I was seven, I had a friend named Nate who I was sometimes taller than, but usually not. (The one good part of hitting puberty a few years later was the delight of no longer being just the tallest girl, but the tallest student overall in the class.) Nate was into *sports*, like *football* and *wrestling*, and I was not, but I also was not about to be outdone in anything, at all, ever. This string of facts and personality—mixed with several strong opinions on how I could absolutely take Nate any and every day—and the echo of my mother's voice saying I was just as good as boys, led to me standing in his nice suburban front yard under the climbing tree, arms resolutely crossed, calmly telling him he had to hit me. There was no particular impetus beyond my fiery blood and need to prove myself, but whatever the reason, I was raring for a fight.

He refused. His mother said he couldn't hit girls, he told me. Obviously, I was a girl.

DOUBLE STANDARD, lit up the neon lights in my head, minus the exact wording because I didn't have the vocabulary for that yet. Still, I knew unfairness when I saw it, and I was out for blood and/or justice. Girls can do anything that boys can! I was *just* as hittable as him!

"You *have* to *hit* me," I implored/protested/yelled, stressing every other word like the worst Shakespearean actor imaginable. "I *told* you to. You *have* to!"

"My mom *said* I can't hit girls," he repeated, which is generally solid advice, but not to a quick-to-anger seven-year-old's ears.

"That's sexist. Your mom is sexist." Before he could get in a retort, I swiftly kicked him in the shins, my light-up Skechers scuffing up his skin.

And that's when he hit me. Tackled me, rather, which was what I had been going for, plus it circumvented his mother's directive. This was one of the unfortunate times when Nate was taller than me, so I did not win the wrestling match, but in my heart, I won the fight.

That was my elementary school contribution to women's rights—a literal fight for equality with misplaced motive but true passion. But I didn't stop there—I continued to be just terrible at being a feminist through middle school, too.

In middle school I was Not Like Other Girls. I was Not Like Other Girls because I read *books* and participated in *fandoms* and absolutely did *not*, God forbid, wear *makeup*. And, unlike Other Girls, I also had a nemesis, though I'm not even sure she knew it. Her name was Sophie (or actually it wasn't, but it's a good enough pseudonym), and I *hated* her.

Our conversations usually played out something like this:

INT: YEARBOOK ROOM, DAY.

EARLY IN THE SCHOOL YEAR. THE ROOM IS FILLED WITH fluorescent lights, motivational posters, and preteens who don't want to be there. MEGAN, budding emo, is seated at a computer, intently pretending that she knows what she's doing with the yearbook software, when she is approached by SOPHIE, popular and trendy.

SOPHIE
(holding a vanilla Starbucks frappuccino)

Oh my God, are you wearing mascara?

MEGAN
(voice quaking with the wrath of a thousand gods)

NO.

SOPHIE
(confused as to why MEGAN sounds as if she has just watched SOPHIE light her homework on fire and steal her lunch money)

Oh, it's just your lashes look really nice.
MEGAN, who refuses to ever look nice or under-stand how to accept a compliment she deems unwor-thy, stalks away with a glare to complain about SOPHIE'S stupid new iPhone 4 or listen to Evanes-cence, this cool indie band no one else has heard of that just really gets her.

TRAUMATIZING, I KNOW.
    I was convinced that I was special, that I was the exception, fighting alone against the impenetrable bastion of teenage girls' egos. But that was *my* ego speaking, my own arrogance convincing myself that I was better because I was different, even if I was neither better nor different. All those other girls read books and complained about

teachers and did everything else I could do; things as superficial as whether I wore makeup or talked about boys never really mattered. By trying to defeat the vague but formidable enemy of teenage girls as a group, I'd fallen into the trap of fighting myself.

Years later, I realized that purchases from Starbucks are not an indicator of someone's moral character (plus their cake pops are overpriced but really good), that Sophie was making an effort to be nice while I was making an effort to be an asshole, and that I should probably stop insulting people for being stereotypical white girls when I, too, am a white girl. I realized that it's probably a good idea to teach your sons not to hit girls, though one can make an exception for a battle-ready one who is quite literally asking for a fight.

Now, at 17, I still don't think I'm a good feminist, but I'm trying. (I can see myself 10 years from now, laughing like "Wow, I really thought [insert common value that will abruptly become outdated in the near future here]?! What an idiot!") I'm learning, and I'm not hating on people for the way society paints them, and I'm not asking Nate (who is now several inches taller than me and a football player) to beat me up. I'm thinking before I act, and I'm trying to be a good feminist and a good person.

And I still do *not* wear mascara, thank you very much, Sophie, but I can take a compliment on my eyelashes now.

MEGAN SULLIVAN, 17, LIVES IN THE WASHINGTON, D.C., AREA with her parents, her two sisters, her dog, and a terrible cat. When she was 13, she decided she intended to be a writer, and a few thousand handwritten, painstaking notebook pages later, here she is, published! Megan spends her free time having strong opinions on everything, avoiding math homework, and talking people's ears off about Ancient Rome.

28

THE WOMAN SHE WAS MEANT TO BE

BY MARY KAY JORDAN FLEMING

"My head is *not* red!" my two-year-old declared from her stroller, eyes wide and back straightened. Not a typical reaction to a stranger's innocent compliment about my beautiful redheaded girl, but then my daughter was not a typical toddler.

Julia sported two tiny clenched fists in her newborn photo, one in the left-jab position. That was our first indication that she would take her place in a long line of strong women in our family, eventually earning the same force-of-nature reputation as the grandmother she never met. I loved seeing the similarities, including their unbridled displays of affection.

Each night at bedtime, Julia offered kisses and declared that her love was as boundless as the universe. "I love you more than a thousand universities!" She asked her dad to kneel by her big-girl bed and give "pats" to help her fall asleep. If his actions became too vigorous, she corrected his technique: "Just light, not hard." If he dozed off, she woke him to resume his post. It was important to follow protocol.

Julia was equally eager to express other desires and opinions. When our large energetic dog dragged her across the soccer field by the leash, she decided that she needed her own, smaller, dog to train. At dinner, she requested a "picky bowl" for dispatching wayward celery or cabbage or other non-approved ingredients. She hand-selected her clothing ensembles each day, including a pink tutu she wore almost constantly for two years. On tutu days, the major fashion decision came down to complementary footwear—everything from flip-flops to gym shoes to cowboy boots, regardless of weather.

My husband, Don, was sometimes exasperated by Julia's appetite for spirited debates. Would there be no opportunities for him to have the last word? I advised him to pick his battles. In the preschool world of green vs. purple pants, and I-open-the-package-in-five-seconds vs. Julia-opens-it-herself-in-five-minutes, there is much more at stake than time and technique.

Toddlers and preschoolers are curious and eager to learn about their world and abilities. We parents find it more expedient to make all the decisions, zip all the zippers, and buckle all the carseats, but children's developmental needs are better served by taking a longer view. What qualities and experiences will prepare an adult woman to solve her own dilemmas, defend her convictions, and advocate on behalf of herself and others? The skills needed to make informed decisions and resist bullying and peer pressure do not emerge overnight; they must be learned and practiced, starting early in life.

Julia's strong feelings and opinions came as a surprise to Don, who claims he was an easy-going and compliant firstborn. That left me— the youngest of five in a family where the choices were to speak up or be overrun by wisecracking older siblings—as the presumed cause of Julia's assertiveness. It didn't help that my brothers egged on my husband in this attribution. Even I recognized our similarities when Julia and her older brother were horsing around in the backseat of the car and Julia piped up in her best sing-song voice, "Helloooo, does anyone care that Stephen is punching me?" Shades of my own childhood.

Any remaining skepticism about our similarities was dispelled in a Mother's Day poem my daughter wrote years later.

People sometimes tell me
They see a resemblance between my mom and me.
If only they could see inside my soul,

There would be no doubt.

Julia's unique sense of style continued even after her two-year love affair with the pink tutu waned. She and her best friend dragged me to the fabric store to recreate the colorful, ruffly-sleeved costumes in Mary-Kate and Ashley Olsen's "Miami" video. The girls performed this song in their satin-and-leotard get-ups so often that they hatched a plan to record a music CD and sell it at our local drug store.

When the time came to choose a dress for First Communion, Julia preferred her own creative imagination to any of the poufy numbers at local department stores. She asked the seamstress across the street to fashion one according to her specifications: white lace top and shimmery skirt connected at a V-waist with an illusion neckline (foreshadowing her wedding dress) adorned by hanging teardrop pearls. Julia was the only girl in second grade to design her own dress and wear a flowered headband instead of a veil.

After the soccer-field incident, Julia succeeded in talking us into getting a second dog. With Meghan, the world's most headstrong bichon, Julia became the youngest handler in her Puppy Kindergarten class. She enjoyed the challenge so much that her first career aspiration was to become a dog trainer. Against some odds, she managed to teach enough obedience for Meghan to earn a Canine Good Citizen Award, complete an agility class, compete in a 4-H dog show, and become a popular therapy dog at a local nursing home.

After mastering dog training, Julia considered careers in pharmacy or law. I advised her to ask her cousin about her career as a paralegal. When I explained the difference between a lawyer and a paralegal, Julia quickly clarified her goal. "Oh, I wanna be the boss of whatever I be."

Julia's peers recognized her leadership and elected her to school president in grade school and senior-class president in high school. Her coaches selected her as captain of the track team because she practiced hard and cheered even harder for her teammates. Together, they went on to earn state titles and school records. She received the Most Distinguished Graduate award at her high-school commencement where the valedictorian later sought out our family for congratulations.

"Whenever I face a hard decision, I just ask myself what Julia would do."

I have long admired my daughter's ability to cultivate friendships, which was never more evident than at a bridal shower hosted by her fiancé's mom. Extended family and friends swarmed me at the door of the church hall. "Please come in, come in. We've been waiting so long to meet you. We love Julia!" My daughter's second family included a mother, two grandmothers, a sister, and dozens of cousins, aunts, friends, and neighbors. Without my even realizing it, she had done what we all hope our children do: She created a supportive network to sustain her marriage and adult life.

Today, Julia is a 27-year-old neuropsychologist-in-training who has earned grants, awards, and a coveted fellowship at a top pediatric hospital. In a recently completed internship, she submitted reports that were so thorough and scholarly her supervisors couldn't believe they were written by an intern. One particularly demanding mentor came to her office to ask, with some skepticism, "Who *are* you?"

That is the question that each of us must answer throughout life in a constant cycle of self-discovery and definition. As she has done all her life, Julia will speak her own truth to provide the answer.

Meanwhile, in this mother's heart, the memories are clear. Julia is the newborn who came out swinging. She is the toddler who corrected a well-meaning elderly woman in the middle of a department store by declaring that red hair did not give her a red head. She is the girl who traded her tutu for soccer and track uniforms. She is the confident college student who navigated foreign countries to study abroad, and the graduate student who ventured out on clinical internship a year early because she was ready to build a career.

Julia is every girl who is lifted up rather than shut down, celebrated rather than stifled, and encouraged to forge her own path with clarity and purpose. She is every woman who is given the chance to be her best self—the strong and capable woman she was always meant to be.

MARY KAY FLEMING IS A PROFESSOR OF PSYCHOLOGY AND WINNER of the 2016 Erma Bombeck Writing Competition for humor. She publishes online at HumorWriters.org, McSweeney's Internet Tendency, Boomer Café, Sammiches & Psych Meds, *and* Pulse: More Voices from the Heart of Medicine, *and contributed to anthologies about loss of a parent* These Summer Months: Stories from the Late Orphan Project, *and sisterhood* In Celebration of Sisters.

29

GIRL POWER SOMETIMES STILL REQUIRED DAD'S ADVICE

BY MANDY WAYSMAN

"**I**f you take him back again, I will beat you and then I will find him and kick his ass."

Words of wisdom from my father. Oh, you didn't read it as advice? You read it as a threat? I guess I can see why, but I intend to convince you that it's not only advice but the best advice I have ever received.

First, I should tell you my father would never beat me. I mean, don't tell him that I know that. He's worked pretty hard at his rough exterior. I hate to be the one responsible for unearthing his sensitive side. He is the best kind of dad. The kind that knows how to do the manly things and will help in a heartbeat with car or house repairs. He cares a lot about his baby girl (me). He doesn't always know the right words to use to portray it, as evidenced above by the crap that spilled out of his mouth when I was bawling. To be fair, my dad's language he thought he was saying, "I love you and don't know why you are allowing this to hurt you. I would beat up anything that hurts you. This is a goshdarn pickle." This isn't an exact translation, but pretty solid if I say so myself. It's probably best now to explore why this advice was required in the first place.

My boyfriend had broken up with me. The boyfriend would be the "him" that was going to get his ass kicked if I took him back. He was my first boyfriend. My first "real" kiss. My first love. My first everything. I must not be saying that right because it meant everything to me at the time, yet as I reread that sentence it's not making me feel the urgency and heartbreak that was palpable for so long. I'm not getting that flutter in my gut with the spicy heat of heartache that travels up the throat into my face. The feelings that I thought I wouldn't ever get on the other side of.

When I was 16, I got a job at Sears. I went in with my friend, Tina. We didn't expect interviews that day. We were simply filling out applications. I may have been trying to put on a good show at attempting to get a job and crossing my fingers it would not pan out. Joke was on us (the standard for life experience) because we filled out the applications and then they wanted to interview us right on the spot. I would like to think that it was because we were so poised and presented ourselves very well. I'm not delusional though, so I'll be straight with you. We were dressed in cutoff jean shorts and tank tops. Classy. We got the jobs. I don't want to belabor this point or brag, but our personalities had a lot to overcome in the interview—and we did. My friend Tina got a job in the shoe department and I was placed in the children's department.

There was a handsome guy in the shoe department with Tina. He was super friendly to everyone. I was shy and reserved, so seeing him so completely at ease chatting with people was both confusing and kind of magical. I needed to get closer to the subject so I could discover what this magic was. I didn't say anything to anyone because I wasn't quite ready to play Peg Bundy to his Al. Important notes include: I had no plan on how to get closer to him, nor did I have any game whatsoever when it came to attracting boys.

Everything changed one night when I got a call at work from Tina. It might even have been at work. (We dialed each other to plan breaks.) It seems like something she would do during that time.

"There is a male specimen that is interested in you," Tina said. She really had a way of making things romantic, huh? Everyone needs a friend like that.

I think that I might have instantly blushed from head to toe. It must have been a slow time at work because I don't remember anyone attempting to pull me back together. No slap across the face with a "Pull yourself together, girl." After that didn't happen I tried not to sound too anxious to know who it was and failed. I said: "Tell me now."

Obviously, the specimen was my very own Al Bundy. I'm not here to rewrite how high school romance goes. So, that was the start of it. Tina had a party at her house where Al and I shared our first kiss on her deck. Her parents still live in that house and I'm sure they think about my first kiss every day. Unless they never knew about the party —in which case, never mind.

After the kiss, Tina asked me how it was. I said, "Lots of tongue." She told him to back off. Because that is what friends who find you male specimens do. They take charge and fix it, especially when you're uncomfortable.

We proceeded to date for three years. It was through my prom, my graduation, and him growing into a man. He graduated a year or two ahead of me. He was in the real world and renting an apartment and house. I did half days through my senior year and spent a lot of time with Al missing out on school things. All kind of cliché. To abandon high school friends, etc...to hang with the older man. I was okay with it at the time. I knew high school wasn't going to be the best time of my life. I "knew" it with all the confidence that a 18-year-old knows everything.

The boyfriend was someone who always had a plan. His plans changed a few times and reversed and then went back to the beginning. There was always a plan, though. I found that was very appealing. My plan was to just get through high school. When that was checked off my list, I had quite the opening in my calendar. Looking back, I don't remember a lot of plans being made together. He seemed to have a lot of his things figured out, but neither of us interjected with what *I* was going to do while he followed his. I would just marry him and move where ever he was and I guess have kids. It was so beautiful because I was so anxious about my future and having to decide. Staying with him was like not having to think or care about myself ever. How refreshing. No dreams to have to fulfill on my end. What a relief. I mean who wants to have the pressure? Just selfish, really...

Now sure, at this age I see that was probably red flags and sirens and smoke telling me that it's not great. At the time though, I wanted to support him. I wanted to support him so I could ignore me. Figuring me out gave me stress. Nodding my head to support him was very easy and perfect.

He broke up with me. Oh, were you blindsided by that coming in right here? Yeah, I was too. It was, I think, a little bit after Christmas, but I'm not sure. I was heartbroken.

Worse than that: I was pathetic.

Truth be told, for Christmas he had gotten me a necklace and there was a minute where I was afraid it was a ring. On some level I knew he wasn't for me. There were nights I told my mom that I didn't think he was supposed to be with me. I just never could break up because I never wanted to hurt him. Turns out not as big a blow to him as I would have thought.

Knowing that I didn't think we were totally meant to be, I still never thought he would leave me. I was completely co-dependent. I didn't want to figure out my life. I called him a lot. I cried a lot. I am so embarrassed. I'm so glad texting and social media weren't things. I can't imagine what kind of shame I would have brought upon myself with that.

Here's the thing. He eventually decided to take me back. That's a weird way to put it because it makes it seem like I did something and needed to make amends to receive forgiveness. No wonder my father wanted to beat me. The boyfriend wanted to break up with me before because he just didn't love me anymore. Just 'cause. The boyfriend's feelings changed. Now a few months later he loved me again. I'm fairly certain I should have seen right through that bullshit. Yet I remember feeling like it was an accomplishment to have won him back.

We dated another few months or year. I never felt at ease again. I always questioned if I was lovable enough now. If he was going to change his mind again. He got a job out of state. About an hour and a half drive from me. I traveled to see and stay with him occasionally. I had a little feeling that he might be cheating or looking. You ever hear someone say the name of someone and just know that there is feeling attached? I had that experience.

He broke up with me again. I carried on again like I had before. It was a learned reaction – and it worked before. I would take my phone to go in my walk-in closet and beg and cry and beg and pathetically try to find ways to talk to him.

He got a new girlfriend (pretty quickly). It was that name I heard him mention before that I had wondered about. He put her on the phone with me once. It stung in a way that I hadn't ever felt before. I was so embarrassed and humiliated. He wasn't doing the humiliation. Truth be told, I was relentless in calling him and looking back it was probably a Hail Mary attempt to be left alone. At the time it was the cruelest thing a person that used to love me could have done.

It was after one of these closet call cry sessions my father saw me and he said the wise words, "If you take him back again I will beat you and kick his ass."

I wish I could say in that moment it clicked. So often though the wisest words have to bounce around before they land. Weeks later I put it together. I was tying myself to someone who didn't care about me. Trying to make their fate intertwine with mine. Making the pain all mine. Loving someone means taking their lumps with them. I was willing to do that. He was definitely not. How is that ever going to work? How would that ever amount to anything? He didn't even care what lumps I was taking in my life (willing to be beat up.) I was a foolish fool that did fool-y things.

So my father was telling me not to be a fool. That this goshdarn pickle was over and I needed to not do things that I would regret. For example, like... hmm... let's say beating someone up. Do I believe that profound lesson was what he was selling in that moment? Yeah. My dad's been pretty solid when he steps in with advice.

The boyfriend married that girl, had kids and then divorced. He contacted me after the divorce and said he regretted our breakup. He would have wanted me back. I was with my husband and happily in love. He went on after that to marry and have more kids. I believe we are both happy now. Neither in danger of getting a can of whoop-ass opened on us.

No matter how good I get at Girl Power, it would never have happened without my Dad's advice. Ladies, don't take a beating (emotionally) for anyone that won't for you. Don't allow yourself the "easy" route of going along for the ride to someone else's plan. It's scary to make your own plan, but it's pretty amazing to feel it when you "make it."

MANDY WAYSMAN IS A FREELANCE WRITER FROM SOUTH DAKOTA. She is the mother of two daughters. She once watched all the episodes of the reality TV show Whisker Wars *and still doesn't know why. She has appeared in* Working Mother *magazine,* Lose the Cape: Never Will I Ever (then I had Kids), *and* The Narcissist's Playbook. *Her work can be found on* Today's Parent, Sammiches and Psych Meds, Scary Mommy, The Week, Parent Map, *and many more parenting websites.*

30

THE SUM ALL FIGURED OUT

BY HARPER KINCAID

I am not your plot twist
Or your manic-pixie-dream-girl,
Solely existing
To make you better.
Nor am I your salvation
In a swishy skirt.
Like some cornflake cinnamon girl who
Walks around campus
Without shoes. You milk fed boys so high.
Greedy even.
Suckling on a fairy tale and a smile.
You boys can't get enough
But sorry, I'm fresh out.

I'm not the woman who brings home the bacon,
All fried up in a pan, served hot, bent over the counter.
Like the porn you sneak at work.
When you think no one's watching.
Is that why you like me in pigtails and Mary Jane shoes?

Man, you must be ten kinds of stupid, and yet,
I'm the one who's not enough?

I'm still not good at math,
But that doesn't mean I don't have the sum all figured out.
That the heart of a soul
Should never be measured by
A number on a tag
Or a grade
Or a ranking on a list.

My worth is not determined by
An algorithm
Or the number of followers
on Instagram.
Although, if I'm going to be really honest,
I wish there were more.
I wish I was more. Or at least enough.

Someday, the brain will convince
What the heart knows to be true.
But until then,
Underneath all my bravado
Is a big bucket of bullshit,
Protecting a heart made raw
By everyone's unmet expectations,
Especially my own.

BORN IN CALIFORNIA AND RAISED IN SOUTH FLORIDA, HARPER KINCAID moved around like a gypsy with a bounty on her head. She been a community organizer and a professional matchmaker. Ms. Kincaid is a published author, known mostly for her romantic comedies, such as The Wonder of You and her new release, Love in Real

Life. She also writes creative nonfiction, poetry, and, most recently, cozy mysteries and suspense.

She is a self-admitted change junkie, but is now happily settled in the cutest 'lil town of Vienna, Virginia, with her wife-whisperer husband, and their two girls.

31

GUIDEPOSTS FOR MY DAUGHTER
AT THE CROSSROADS

BY LESLIE GAAR

D ear Daughter,
You are nine now, fully halfway through the time it is supposed to take me to "raise" you. Your first nine years were dirty diapers and potty training, wobbly first steps and equally-wobbly first dance classes. And while we don't yet know exactly what this next half will bring, we do know that the end of it will see you setting out to face the world on your own. So while I still have you here with me, close by my side, at the crossroads of child and young woman, there are some things I want you to know.

People will judge you by impossible beauty standards. They will tell you you aren't tall enough, or you're too tall. You're not thin enough, or you're too thin. You need makeup, or you look like a clown. Soon, too soon, you will start to question your beauty, and I don't just mean your looks. At this point in your short life the only change you would make to your body would be the addition of a mermaid tail, but soon you will be tempted to pick yourself apart, piece by piece.

But they don't know that "Beauty" was the name of the melody drummed out into the world the second your heartbeat thumped through that ultrasound machine and into my waiting ears. The beauty of that sound, of that incredible gift slowly growing inside me, was lovelier than anything that could be found in the pages of a magazine, no matter how glossy the cover. That wonderfully wild, untamed song belongs to you alone, and its radiance can't be squeezed out of a tube or plucked off a shelf in a store.

People will make you believe your body's sole function is to be a dispenser of pleasure. In time, your body will be constantly evaluated, commented on, degraded, legislated, and maybe even violated by those who inexplicably think they have the right to do so. They will at once praise you for its appearance and crucify you for it based on nothing but their own selfish whims. They will try to make you forget that your body is a palace more wondrous than any built by human hands, and that it is ruled by one, and one alone.

But they weren't with you in the NICU during those small, anxious hours of a Texas morning nine years ago as your body, brand new and marble pink, fought and rested and then fought some more. They can't fathom the strength your body possessed, even when it consisted of fewer than six pounds. To be sure, your body is capable of pleasure in all its forms, but leaving it at that would be laughable. Creation and destruction, work and play, joy and pain, struggle and ease- these are only a few of the abilities already coursing through your veins.

People will demand that you keep quiet in countless ways, some more subtle than others. They will say you're not smart enough, that you're using the wrong words, the wrong tone of voice, the wrong moment, that you hold the wrong viewpoint. They will put words into your mouth and laugh your admonitions off. They will belittle the things you do say, wondering at your insistence on having an opinion at all. They will reward others who play their game, making you question your own voice.

But they don't know that you come from a long line of noisy women who refused to be silenced, and that you took your place in that line as soon as you came screaming into existence. Those women passed on to you a crown of outspokenness, encrusted with jewels of bravery and stubbornness and tenacity. The price of this crown is high, I must tell you. There will be times when you want nothing more than to take it off and just fit in. Don't. There will be times when you think you have lost it completely. You haven't. There will be times when it seems too snug or too loose. It isn't. It is as much a part of you as your wild, curly hair.

People will define your worth by what you can do for others. They will teach you an equation that places your womanhood in direct proportion to your ability to maintain a clean house, wash clothes, prepare meals, and produce and care for children. They will tell you these things are in your nature so many times that you will think something is wrong with you if the scent of fabric softener doesn't set you on fire. They will guilt you into this role of servant, making it seem far more important than any secret desire your heart whispers.

But they don't know that your hands, once chubby and small, now slender and elongated, have bigger aspirations than to fold endless piles of laundry. The books you curl up with on rainy days detail adventures of fairies and witches, not shiny kitchen sinks and perfectly vacuumed floors. You dream of becoming a vet, a ballerina, a chef, and a mommy, all in one spectacularly jumbled-up fantasy. Your worth is wrapped up in these dreams and in your "youness." Don't let anyone tell you differently.

I know these words mean little to you now, dear Daughter, but someday they will. And so, for now, my wish is that they seep into your skin and filter into your bones. Let them stay there, dormant, until you have need of them. Remember them when life becomes more complicated than it is just now, when your soul is crying out with a dissonance you don't understand. And just in case these words leave you, in case you forget, I'll be here to remind you of them, now, then, and always.

Love, Mommy

LESLIE GAAR IS A WRITER, EDUCATOR, AND PERFORMER WHOSE WORK has appeared in The Washington Post, Scary Mommy, Babble, and TODAY Parents' "Funniest Parents on Facebook." She is currently *writing her first book because, honestly, life as a mother of three, (twins and a singleton), just felt way too easy, and she wanted to kick things up a notch. Leslie blogs at lesliegaar.com, and can be found on Facebook, Twitter, and Instagram, particularly if she's avoiding work. She lives in Austin, Texas, with her family in a house that will never, ever be free of clutter.*

❧ 32 ❧

BETWEEN BREATHS

BY MIRANDA RAYE

One...

"**W**ill you help deliver my baby?" The question was asked casually over coffee. A bystander might have thought my best friend was asking to borrow a cute top.

I nearly spit out my coffee. "What?"

"You know Randy is still out West for work. I'm confident he'll be back in time, but you know me. I like to be prepared." She flashed me her winning smile. "Will you be my back-up plan?"

Our adult friendship of ten years had begun at work. We were rookie high school teachers, fresh out of college, struggling to stay a day ahead of our students. I was going through some personal issues, willingly isolating myself from others. I remember watching Kathy in the staff lounge during lunch, mesmerized by her eternal optimism, laughing with fellow teachers as I silently munched on my PB&J.

I decided to send her an email which amounted to, "My life sucks right now. I could use a positive person in my life. Will you be my friend?"

She kept a copy and, four years later, read it at my wedding.

We have been through a lot. Bad breakups. Divorce. Diagnoses.

Premature birth. Death. We were roommates. Maids of honor. We were each other's cheerleaders through every event, both joyful and sad.

I was ready to be a part of another joyful moment.

"Of course I will!" I gave her a hug and then we went back to laughing and gossip.

Two...

"KATHY SAID THE CONTRACTIONS AREN'T TOO BAD. SHE'S GOING TO drive herself to the hospital."

"Like hell she is!" My husband proceeded to do an abrupt one-eighty in our Jeep Patriot and floor it to Kathy's house.

We were headed home from a Spartan football game, sleepy from sun and tailgating when Kathy called to say I "shouldn't be alarmed" but she was having some "really close contractions."

She was three weeks early and her husband, Randy, was still in North Dakota with no flight home. We were in Michigan.

It was go time.

Within minutes, my husband was dropping me off at Kathy's condo.

"I'll keep you updated," I told him, "but I have no idea how long I'll be gone. Give the boys a hug and kiss goodnight for me."

"I will." He squeezed my hand. "Take care of Kathy."

Kathy greeted me at the door, her face one of calm serenity in typical Kathy fashion. "I just need to take care of a few things..."

I pulled gently on her arm. "Let's go."

Three...

THE 30-MINUTE DRIVE TO THE HOSPITAL FELT OKAY. WHILE SHE WAS having strong contractions, she managed to keep her spirits up. In fact, we had a great laugh when I wheeled her in to the hospital and a sweet old lady looked over at us and said, "You look like such a happy couple."

In spite of the shared laugh, the absence of Randy hovered over us, leaving a flicker of fear in Kathy's eyes. As soon as we were in the hospital room, the first thing she said was, "My husband isn't here. How long can we wait?"

Kathy got her wish. We waited. And waited.

After a few hours, it was determined she was not yet ready to have the baby. When? They couldn't say, but when Kathy asked if we could go back home, they agreed. Fantastic! We had just found out Randy had secured a flight that would have him back in Michigan late the next morning. It was only seven in the evening now. He would make it.

Capitalizing on our good fortune, we decided to relive our lives as former roommates and order our two staples—B-Dubs and Cold Stone. Why we thought spicy wings and dairy was a good idea when she was having pre-labor contractions, I'll never know. With our take-out strewn across her condo coffee table, we ate, laughed, and enjoyed a trashy romantic comedy. It felt like old times.

As the night wore on, the conversation veered towards the more serious. Kathy asked to hear more about the story of my first son's birth. She had heard most of it before, but then I shared something more intimate.

"I'll never forget looking at Connor, then looking at my parents and thinking, Wow. *This* is how much you love me? I had no idea." I smiled at the memory. It was such a simple revelation, yet it had changed everything for me.

Four...

WE DECIDED I SHOULD DEFINITELY STAY THE NIGHT AT HER PLACE. We didn't want her to be alone until Randy got there. Her parents lived a couple of hours north and were on their way down as well. Soon, Kathy would be surrounded by her family.

It was almost midnight when I rested my head on the spare bedroom pillow. Two minutes later, I heard my phone ringing. It was Kathy, calling me from her room.

I had never heard her voice sound so strained before. "We have to go...now."

I don't remember getting her into the car. What I do remember is driving 90 mph on the dark, empty highway, adrenaline and the after-effects of spicy wings coursing through my body. Kathy was moaning beside me, eyes closed, her hand clutching the door handle for dear life.

Five...

NO CUTE COMMENTS ABOUT WHAT A HAPPY-LOOKING COUPLE WE were this time. It felt like a lifetime ago we had been in the hospital, even though it had only been about five hours. We were greeted imme-diately, and Kathy was quickly put through the rigmarole of hospital gown, IV, and cervical check.

Waiting was no longer an option.

Kathy and I are modest women. When given the choice between a form-flattering top or an oversized hoodie, the hoodie reigns supreme. Like most women, we have a love-hate relationship with our bodies.

Delivering a baby together changed everything. All of those predis-posed fears about our bodies simply didn't matter anymore. Kathy was about to give birth, to literally bring life to the world through her body. And I was going to bear witness.

Stretch marks and dimpled skin can't hold a candle to that.

At first, we were awkward with each other. I felt clumsy, but my hands quickly took over and created their own kind of choreography. Squeeze Kathy's hand. Feed her ice chips. Rub her back. Repeat.

I acquired a newfound respect for my own husband in that room. Being Kathy's birthing coach was by no means as strenuous as giving birth (I had already given birth two times myself and knew there was no comparison), but still, I was struck by the sheer exhaustion of watching her strain and struggle, the feel of her hand grasping mine with a strength I never knew she had until that moment. She chose no epidural. That alone impressed me (I had taken it the first chance I could).

Time lost meaning that night. It comes in flashes.

Frantic texts from friends demanding updates.

Sweat.

Chatting with her parents in the waiting room. "No worries! She's doing great!"

The metallic smell of blood.

Her mother wearing a cheery yellow blouse.

Their faces, bearing excitement and fear and anxiousness, the faces of soon-to-be grandparents.

Stained sheets.

On the phone with Randy. "You need to be here! How much longer?"

Kathy hyperventilating, both in pain and exhaustion.

"Just breathe. Slowly, in through your nose, then out through your mouth."

Thankful she doesn't scratch out my eyes or shout obscenities for such feeble advice.

Dizzy exhaustion.

I lost track of how many hours we had been awake.

She tried every position possible. On her back. Standing. Crouched. Walking.

At first, she didn't seem to mind the delay. After all, she was still holding out for that small hope that Randy would make it.

Time was an ironic tyrant. We longed for his tyranny to end, yet were desperate to hold out a little longer.

After nearly eight hours of laboring, Kathy was finally told she had to have a C-section, and it would have to happen immediately. Devastated, tears ran down Kathy's face. Her pushing had been in vain.

Randy would not make it in time to see the birth of his first child.

Six...

I LEFT THE ROOM TO INFORM HER PARENTS AND JUST BROKE DOWN. It was unintentionally cruel as they immediately thought something was wrong.

"No, no, she's okay, she's fine. I'm just so disappointed for her! It's not fair!" As I cried, her father held me.

"It'll be okay," he told me. "She's strong."

"Yes, yes she is."

As I made my way back to the room, I became acutely aware of how ill-prepared I was to help Kathy with this phase of her delivery. Both of my children had come naturally; getting a C-section was a whole new realm.

They took her away to prep her. I remember sitting in that empty room, silent, mentally preparing myself for what was to come. After what felt like hours, but was only minutes, the nurse came to retrieve me and walked me back to the surgical room.

Seven...

IT WAS COLD. KATHY WAS LYING FLAT ON HER BACK WITH HER ARMS extended, the metal table looking harsh against her hospital gown and bare skin. A sheet hung vertically from the ceiling, shielding the lower half of her body. I was thankful for the face mask covering my look of fear.

"Where do I stand?" I asked awkwardly.

"Sit here on this stool and hold her hand. Don't look behind the sheet."

"Okay."

I held Kathy's hand, still strong. She had Randy on speakerphone. His plane was just touching down. He would be arriving soon. So close, yet too late.

Eight...

THEN THE SHAKING BEGAN. IT SCARED ME, BUT IT SCARED KATHY more. Her whole body started convulsing.

"Normal," we were told, but there was nothing normal about it for us. I remember her grip becoming firmer.

It was shocking how quickly the baby came after the hours she had endured.

"Here he is! A healthy baby boy!" the doctor exclaimed as she held him up for us to see.

"I can't stop shaking." Kathy's eyes were wide with fear. "I don't want to drop him. You hold
him."

"Me?" I was aghast. What right did I have to hold her child first? "No, I can't."

"Please." Her eyes met mine. She smiled. "It's okay."

The nurse handed him to me gently. I remember his cone-shaped head, wrinkled red face, and delicate hands. He was perfect.

"Welcome, Bradley."

It was not long before Kathy's shaking subsided and she was able to hold him. I felt a
surge of relief as I passed him over to her. This was her moment, not mine. Yet, here we were, sharing this joyful moment together.

Nine...

BACK IN THE HOSPITAL ROOM, I STOOD BESIDE HER AS SHE LEARNED to nurse him. Her parents
joined us, their faces in awe as they gazed upon their first grand-child. It was a quiet, beautiful moment—a mother looking down at her daughter as her daughter looks down at her son.

Kathy let out a little gasp, then met my eye. "You were right," she said, her eyes glistening. "I had no idea." She grasped her mother's hand, gazing up at her adoringly.

I quietly left, both as participant and witness to the miracle that is being a woman.

Ten.

MIRANDA RAYE IS A HIGH SCHOOL ENGLISH AND THEATER TEACHER *in Southeastern Michigan where she lives with her husband and two young boys. Her blog, Mommy Catharsis, is about raising a child with autism. She has also written for* Scary Mommy, Sammiches and Psych Meds, Mamalode, The Mighty, *and* Finding Cooper's Voice. *Connect with her on Facebook, Instagram, and Goodreads.*

❧ 33 ❧

WONDER WOMEN—THE NEXT
GENERATION

BY WHITNEY DINEEN

R aising girls is a journey. Much like climbing Mt. Kilimanjaro stark naked, with one leg, no food, covered in only honey and optimism is a journey. In other words, it's treacherous, wonderful, exhilarating, and possibly deadly—the jury's still out on the last one.

Being a girl myself, I know how important it is to guide my daughters and instill confidence in them. In a world that's going to try to tear them down, I need them to know they are the only ones who can do that. No other person has that power, unless they give it to them.

So, I tell them, "Believe in yourself, believe in other people, believe in magic. The world is a miraculous, undiscovered mass of possibility and potential, and it's your job to help unleash that splendor. Go forth and kick some bootay!"

What I don't tell them, and only because they're so young, is that a large chunk of the planet feeds on the misery and insecurity of others —everyone from mean girls to future bosses, politicians, and Hollywood will tell them they aren't smart enough, talented enough, thin enough, pretty enough...the list goes on. Sadly, they'll learn that on their own and it's my job to be there to tell them not to trust the naysayers.

So far, my daughters are so full of "Girl Power" and confidence in their gender, they've started to actually pity boys. My youngest, Hope, is seven. She's oft heard opining, "I feel sorry for so-and-so (insert boy's name here)."

Inevitably, I ask, "Why?"

She responds, "Because of the fashion! He doesn't get to wear great clothes and earrings. He'll never have boobs or a closet full of high heels. Plus, he eats his boogers on the playground. A girl would never do that."

So, I ask her about her two particular male friends, and why she's friends with them. To which she answers, "They're sweet little boys. They can't help being gross."

My older daughter, Margery, while still vigorously in love with being a girl, is a little more tolerant of the opposite sex. She's nine and beginning to see that boys have their place in the world. Although she often complains about the stupidity of men *back in the day*. "Can you believe there was a time when women weren't allowed to vote? Can you believe we haven't had a woman president? I hope they're not waiting for me. I haven't decided if I want the job, yet." Never has it occurred to her that she won't be the president if she chooses to be.

When the male-bashing starts to get out of hand, I ask them about their Daddy and Poppy, reminding them, "You know, Daddy and Poppy are boys."

"But they're not stupid boys. They were smart enough to marry you and Moses." Moses is the name my daughters call my mom.

Hope inserts, "I've never seen Daddy eat his boogers. Plus, he lets me read to him every night and he teaches me about history. *And* he's a great basketball player!"

I'm trying to raise my daughters to be comfortable with themselves, proud in their abilities, and tolerant of the world around them. I want them to grow up feeling sure they can do or be anything they want and to know they have my full support in their endeavors.

Will they encounter people who try to make them feel less-than? Will they work for people who don't see their worth? Will they ever feel insecure? The answers are all the same. Hell yeah, cause that's just life, folks. That's part of everyone's journey, man or woman. It's how they process those experiences that will dictate their success.

Our girls are learning the world is often perplexing. Fairness and kindness do not always win out. So, we're teaching them that when they notice something that makes them mad or upset, it's up to them to step forward and make a difference. Complaining is never the answer, action is.

Margery is ruled by compassion and a desire to make the world a better place. At nine, she's already succeeded. Three years ago, she spearheaded a campaign to collect fifty purses and backpacks for the homeless. With the help of our friends, we filled them with food, hats, gloves, scarves, toiletries, and a small amount of money. Margery drew a picture of an angel and wrote a beautiful letter of encouragement that we enclosed in each.

Hope will defend the downtrodden to the death, although her actions are a little more aggressive than Margery's. For instance, if you're unkind to someone in her presence or treat them unfairly, you had better protect your kneecaps. She probably won't ask you nicely to change your ways. But for your own safety, you should.

Both girls were behind me writing a children's book called *The Friendship Bench* that they, along with their classmates, illustrated. One hundred percent of the proceeds are donated to our PTC to be used for acts of kindness.

I know my daughters will have their hearts broken and be the recipients of unfair treatment, but that isn't because they're girls. It's a human condition. My job is to make sure they know that standing up for themselves is the answer. They may not always get the job they deserve. They may not always get paid what they should. But they should always know their worth.

I'm not looking forward to wiping their tears as they learn some of the ugly truths about the world. But I'll tell you this, I'm not going to let them wallow in self pity. Things change when people demand change. I'm teaching my girls that they have a voice and an obligation to be part of the change. I'm teaching them to be kind and courageous. Other than that, it's a crap shoot.

Since their births, I've been cobbling together a list of things that I think is mandatory for my future Wonder Women to learn. It evolves on almost a daily basis, but the current rendition reads as follows:

- You are no better than any other person on this planet.
- The Karmic wheel is real! Seriously, only put out there what you want to come back to you because it will, tenfold, like a hurricane in the shape of a fist or a kiss, your choice.
- You *can* wear white before Memorial Day.
- Underwear is not optional. You can recover from the embarrassment of torn pants if you're wearing undies, but there's no coming back from commando.
- Things are only placeholders for the important stuff, like kindness and love.
- Whining is never productive.
- French fries can solve most problems.
- Marry a person who makes you laugh.
- Your mistakes don't define you. They're no more than a stairway to growth.
- Be loyal.
- Don't take any crap.
- Don't be an a-hole.
- Swiss buttercream is often a better choice than American buttercream as it won't overwhelm the palate with sweetness.
- Be the kind of friend you want to have.
- Don't be afraid to be vulnerable.
- Always sing at the top of your lungs to Queen, even if you sound awful. It's good for the soul.

NOW THAT MY DAUGHTERS ARE ON THE PLANET, AND NOT JUST imaginary, I feel the weight of responsibility like an elephant standing on my neck. I want to do right by them and make sure I equip them with everything they need to succeed. It's terrifying and invigorating at the same time, and I can't wait to continue my journey with them.

WHEN NOT ACTIVELY RAISING HER GIRLS, WHITNEY DINEEN CAN *often be found organizing their drawers, chasing chickens around the backyard, or hiding in a closet to swear. Dineen is an award-winning author of nonfiction humor, romantic comedies, and middle grade fiction. Her memoir,* Motherhood, Martyrdom & Costco Runs, *won a gold medal at the International Readers' Favorite Awards in Non-fiction/Humor and was a finalist at the Book Excellence Awards. Whitney loves to connect with her readers. You can find her at whitneydineen.com, Facebook, or Twitter.*

❦ 34 ❦

RAISING A STRONG DAUGHTER
WHO IS COMPLETELY HERSELF IS
MY ULTIMATE GOAL

BY KATIE BINGHAM SMITH

I grew up in the '80s hearing things like "You can never be too skinny or too rich," and "Nothing tastes as good as skinny feels." Perhaps people think they are just words, but try telling that to an 11-year-old girl who has developed earlier than all of her friends, is wearing almost a C cup, and has hips that could bear children. I took that shit to heart. I believed it. I felt it in my soul, and so did all my friends, by the way. I'm pretty sure those phrases affected many females the same way – in a negative one.

To be skinny and rich was to matter; it meant you'd made it. And if you weren't thin you weren't strong; you had zero willpower and, well, you didn't deserve to be validated. You pretty much sucked.

We've made some progress since then, but a few months ago as I was shopping with my daughter, she held up a tank that said, "Strong is the new sexy," as she asked if she could buy it, I was cringing.

Not because I don't think strong can be sexy—I do. But being strong has this physical and mental connotation associated with it. I'm not talking about muscles either.

"What do you think being strong means?" I asked her. As she thought for a moment she said she thought it meant being able to stand up for yourself and not care what other people thought about you.

While I agree, I've learned a few things about being strong since my divorce happened a year ago—our horrible circumstances are always teaching us something if we choose to accept the lesson. I've cried almost every day since my ex-husband and I decided to split. Does that make me look strong to my kids? I don't know, I've never asked them. But I'm thinking instead of asking them I need to tell them that being vulnerable, crying, and asking for help is what makes you a strong person, too.

At first, I tried to hide my blubbering self by only allowing myself to cry in the bathroom while I had the door shut and the shower running, then I got my water bill.

I'd cry in the car after dropping them off at their father's house, but if I had a date that night, had plans to meet up with friends, or was taking myself out for a Diet Coke and a shopping spree, I'd look like a hot mess, so that wasn't working either.

I didn't want my crying to be another reason to add to the list of all the other things I felt I was doing to screw up my kids' lives, so I was hiding it, which is the opposite of what I should've been doing.

Before I knew it, I had no control when they tears would come and I was getting really tired of trying to hold it in to appear "strong" for my kids all the time. I just needed to be myself. I am an oversensitive over-thinker who talks too much. I grew up constantly feeling like I had to censor myself or overcompensate to make other people comfortable. I'd shut my mouth when I wanted to disagree, hold in emotions – and now as a woman in her 40s, I realize this has benefited no one.

That part of me is slowing being peeled away layer by layer because I'll be damned if I am going to teach my daughter you make other people feel good about themselves by compromising your needs, stuffing your emotions, and censoring yourself. How can I raise my daughter to be a fierce, strong independent female if I'm afraid to shed a tear for fear it will make me look like I can't handle life and I don't know what I'm doing?

The truth is, I have no fucking clue what I'm doing. This single life of mine is new, and scary, and I've never done this before. But I show up every day for her and her brothers. I am not going to fall on my face *every day*, but I can promise there *will* be days all I can manage is a face plant in a bag of chips with a squishy sofa supporting me. It's okay not to know what's next, or to not appear strong and in control—it's more than okay, it called being human.

Being brave and strong and all these things that are deemed as the "new pretty" don't mean your aren't ever afraid. They mean you are afraid, but you are willing to put yourself in an uncomfortable spot because you know that's what is right. And you keep doing it because despite how hard it is, you know it's the best way for your to show up for those you love, and more importantly, it's about showing up for yourself.

I will never tell my daughter to cheer up if she's really freaking pissed. I will never make her feel like she needs to smile if she doesn't feel like it; it's her body. If she doesn't feel like smiling, she shouldn't any more than if she should hold hands with someone she doesn't want to touch. If she needs to cry every day for a year, then so be it. That's what she should do.

While these messages about being brave and strong and all are much better than letting our girls know they are only worthy if they are rich and thin, I want my daughter to know being herself is the new pretty, or sexy, or beautiful—or whatever. And there are going to be days when she doesn't give a damn about being pretty, and she doesn't need to stuff that emotion, either.

I want her to be herself at all costs, even if it is hard and makes those around her uncomfortable. Because what will happen if I don't teach her that all the things which make her unique will slowly be stripped away because she's trying to live up to someone else's defini-tion of how a woman should be. And from a woman who has been there—she, and all the other young girls walking this earth, deserve so much more.

KATIE BINGHAM-SMITH HAD THREE KIDS IN THREE YEARS AND crafts her ass off in order to stay sane. You can often find her wearing faux leather pants, drinking Diet Coke, and paying her kids to play with her hair and rub her feet. She is a staff writer for Scary Mommy *and regular contributor to* Babble, SheKnows, Grown and Flown, *and* Mom.me. *Feel free to harass her on Instagram @katiebinghamsmith and Facebook @Katiebinghamsmithwriter.*

35

FREE BLEEDING: AN EXPERIENCE

BY MOLLY SANDLER

I have this theory that if every woman on earth refused to wear any products when they were on their periods—what would be called "free bleeding"—then tampons, pads, and all other period-related products would be untaxed within, like, two hours. Honestly, I think they'd probably be free, since many men (including my father) seem to have a major problem with anything involving a period, especially the blood part (and the cramps part, and the mood swings part...).

During a "situation" in the eighth grade, I found out that if you tell anyone that you're bleeding out of your vagina, even if this bleeding is purely accidental, they will let you do whatever you need to do, just so they can avoid discussing anything remotely near the topic, or the blood you are currently bleeding.

And this story is where I tell you that I was once, in fact, a free bleeder, and have lived to tell the tale. So if it happens to you, you will too. And maybe we'll even get free tampons out of it.

Here's what happened...

It was a typical hot day in June, and I woke up with a visit from Aunt Flo. So naturally, as one does, I go put in a tampon. I don't know if this was a known fact for everyone except me, but apparently a tampon can be kinda diagonal up there and just not catch any blood at all if you put it in slightly wrong, quite possibly leading to free bleeding. But obviously that would never happen to me, right? Wrong.

Very wrong.

It was sixth period, and my chair was feeling... sticky. We all know the struggle of leg sweat on hot days, so that's clearly what I assumed it was. But just to make sure, I looked down to confirm. Instead of cutoffs and slightly sweaty thighs, I saw a literal crime scene going on between my legs.

We're talking at least six murder victims worth of blood. Possibly seven. I cannot explain in words the horror that was happening to me right then. Everyone reading this, take the worst period situation you can possibly imagine, and multiply it times ten. Then another ten. And did I have any sort of product on me? No, no I did not. So me, being the strong independent woman that I am, immediately turned to my friend Laura next to me and simply pointed at my crotch so she could tell me what to do about it.

Her helpful advice was a quick grab of the arm and a hissed, "We need to get you to the bathroom *now*. I'll bring you a pad from my locker on the way."

I come from a school with very strict bathroom rules, like what I imagine the rules must be like in prison. You can't leave the classroom to go to the bathroom if anyone else is out already, you can't go during the first, or last, 15 minutes of class, and you definitely cannot go with a friend. Unfortunately, Laura and I were going to break all three of these rules by leaving.

I asked my teacher Mr. Smith if we could leave. As expected, he basically assumed we were joking by even asking him this and told us to go back to our seats. That's when I was like, "Uh no, we need to go together," adding, "It's an emergency, I swear."

But since that's what everyone who wants to leave class with their friend says, he responded with a strong no. After probably three minutes of me pleading with him and being met with continued unsympathetic looks from Mr. Smith, I decided I was utterly and completely done with his patriarchal nonsense, and did what needed to be done.

I pulled my shirt slightly away from my body so he could see the crimson tide I'd been attempting to conceal up until this point during our prolonged conversation.

His entire attitude completely changed within half a second. Guy couldn't get me out of his classroom fast enough. "Oh. Oh. *Ohhhhh.* Oh no. I wasn't aware it was that type of situation. Of course you two can leave. Do you need anyone else? Should I call a doctor? Here's the hall pass. Here, take two. Take as much time as you need."

As we were about to leave he even yelled out a final helpful sugges-tion, "Actually, don't even bother coming back, there's only like ten minutes left in this class anyway."

Laura and I took the passes and made a stop at her locker for a pad before continuing to the bathroom.

The first thing Laura said was, "God, Molly, do you even have any blood left in you?"

We concluded I had no choice but to change my shorts ASAP, but of course I didn't have gym clothes with me that day, and making the situation even better, neither did Laura. Then the bell rang (Yay! Super-helpful timing!) and the only rule at my school more strict than the bathroom policy was the not-being-late-to-class policy.

I slowly walked to my next class, desperately hoping I'd run into someone whose clothes I could borrow. Luckily, my sometimes-we-interact, occasionally, maybe, friend Angela was walking practically next to me, and we happened to share our next class.

Without even giving her an explanation, I pulled her towards the lockers and showed her my own personal bloodbath situation. Without me even asking, she immediately insisted I take her gym shorts, since my shorts were clearly unwearable at that point. My only obstacle between me and cleanliness was our next teacher, Ms. Link.

Based on how the last bathroom request I made went, I decided I wasn't going to waste any time reasoning with her. I told her I was having an emergency and needed to go to the bathroom with Angela, and showed her my shorts without waiting for her response to my request. Giving me a disgusted face, Ms. Link told us to hurry up and be back in, like, two minutes, leading me to the realization that female teachers can be assholes about periods, too.

Long story short, I changed, returned to class with Angela, and was saved from the worst and most embarrassing moment of my young life. But all in all, still pretty much one of my worst days ever.

The one small bright spot was that I now knew that Angela, even though she wasn't even close to being my best friend, was absolutely willing and able to take on the BFF role when I really needed her help. And hopefully Angela knew I would do the same for her or anyone else who needed me to share a pad or a pair of shorts because their rogue tampon did not do its only job.

I should also add that when I got home and told my mother the horrific story in all its gory details, she immediately took me out for ice cream, as much as I wanted, with literal whipped cream and a cherry on top.

In conclusion, free bleeding is a very effective way to get things to go your way in school, make new friends, and get a parent to buy you ice cream. I ten out of ten recommend it for everyone considering the idea.

MOLLY SANDLER WAS BORN IN NEW YORK CITY AND IS NOW A HIGH school student living in New Jersey with her family and dog, Daisy.

❧ 36 ❧

FINDING MYSELF

BY JULIA BOZZA

When high school students complain about their lives, adults always respond with, "Stop complaining. Wait until you are an adult with *real* problems." And, while there is no doubt that the problems of being an adult carry a much different weight, being in high school today is still a challenge. Anyone who has ever been a teenager once understood the social pressure to make friends and be popular. Countless high school students live those four years in envy of the "popular kids" and their epic parties and perfect lives. For a while, it seemed like I was being set up to become one of them. It felt like the high school dream was being handed to me. Freshman year I found myself in the middle of a friend group of kids who were smart, athletic, and actually nice. It was wonderful, I felt like I was in with the in-crowd—and for a freshman, it was an amazing feeling. However, at some point during our freshman year, these friends started to throw parties. They were fun parties, but they often left me uncomfortable. Even though I enjoyed the get-togethers, I hit a point where it felt like instead of being a part of the group, I was looking in from the outside. I found myself becoming unhappy with my life, specifically with my friends.

Was there something wrong with me? I was a part of a group

containing some of the most well-known students in my grade, a group that many students wanted to be a part of. Why was I so unhappy? Trapped, I continued to attend the parties and get-togethers, wanting to stay in the "popular group," but in the back of my mind, I knew that this wasn't where I wanted to be. I hit a point where I was unhappy all the time, spending countless nights stressing over how alone I felt until one day I had a sudden realization. All the advice my parents had given me about friendship had finally sunk in, and a part of me began to listen. I realized that life isn't about having the most friends or being in the most well-known group in school—it's about finding people you are happiest with. In that moment, I realized that I was trapped in a prison, one I had made for myself, by defining myself by the people with whom I hung out.

I wasn't always disappointed in my friend group, I was happy for a long time before high school. In third grade, my family moved, causing me to switch schools, leaving behind a lot of my old friends, and I needed to make new ones. Throughout the rest of elementary school, I had a few friends, but I couldn't help feeling jealous of all the people who had "best friends" that they had known since kindergarten, something I would never have in a new school. Finally, middle school rolled around and my friends from third to fifth grade were scattered into different classes and I was alone once again. Going into middle school, I knew only one girl in my classes. I had taken tennis lessons with her when we were younger so we kind of knew each other, and we clicked immediately. We had most of our classes together, ate lunch together, and she introduced me to all of her friends. By the middle of seventh grade, we had become a part of a new friend group of girls in our math class. We were a tight-knit group. We all stayed friends through the rest of middle school and I was overjoyed that I had finally found a friend group, true friends who wouldn't disappear on me. This was everything I had dreamed of socially. But every good thing must come to an end, and my social life began to unravel with the dawn of high school.

My group and I stayed close throughout freshman year, and our tiny group of girls had expanded into one large group of people from all different middle schools. One of my friends began to throw parties during the holiday season for the group. The parties weren't huge, but they were always posted all over social media afterward and people would talk about them for the rest of the week. People would tell me how they wished they were invited to her parties and how they wanted to be in the friend group with us. Despite how happy I had been through middle school I remained socially insecure, so, I admit that I somewhat enjoyed the feeling of having people look up to me and my friends. I was well-liked and it seemed as though my friends and I were gradually becoming more and more popular.

Then came my sophomore year and everything changed. The parties continued, but the focus of the conversations changed and I became more uncomfortable and out of my element. While I still had fun with my friends, I felt anxious being there and I'm sure it was evident. I began to feel like an outsider in this group that I had always enjoyed being a part of. Outside of school the girls formed smaller groups within our large one and began to exclude other girls, including myself. Technology certainly played a role as there were a dozen group text chats that were running, and even though everyone was not included in all of them, my friends would mention the other group chats in the larger ones. The feeling was, "not only are we excluding you, but we are also going to make sure you *know* you are being exclud-ed." Being my anxious and "don't want to make waves" self, I continued to stay passive and allowed my emotions get tossed around by the girls I thought were my "good friends." I realized that the amazing social life I thought I had was just a facade and my heart was broken. As most teenagers do, I had identified myself by the friend group I was in. If I wasn't one of them, who was I? My parents could see how unhappy I was and would suggest that I find new friends if these ones were only bringing me sadness and disappointment, but I didn't know how. For years, I had created a tunnel vision view of my social life and when I imagined leaving, I couldn't envision myself actually belonging in any other group. I felt trapped. My sadness grew and, finally, I found myself in the depths of a depression that I was sure I would not be able to crawl out of.

However, I continued to talk to my parents and continued to imagine a different future for myself. And I also began to realize that my friends weren't bad or evil. We simply had different priorities and different ideas about what friendship should be. And little by little, I began to care less about what they thought. When they would all be going to a party that I wasn't invited to, I found that I didn't care quite as much anymore. And sometimes, when I was invited, I would decline. I remembered all of the things that I liked about myself and realized that I wasn't going to spend my life alone if I chose a different group of friends, or even decided to be part of multiple groups of friends. I could still be friends with these people without having them be my everything. I began to be happy again. And once I opened myself up to that happiness, new opportunities for friendship came my way.

In my drawing class, there was only one other sophomore, and at the beginning of the year, we sat together to avoid sitting alone. While I somewhat knew her from theatre and middle school, we were not "good friends." She was also in my history class and she sat with her best friend in the front of the room. They were always smiling and laughing and having a great time together while I sat in the back of the room with a few girls from my friend group who consistently excluded me from the conversation. In mid-January, this girl and her friend approached me before class and invited me to sit with them. I would be lying if I said I wasn't surprised. They barely knew me, yet somehow had sensed my exclusion and actually *wanted* me to join them. I accepted and they happily welcomed me to their table. I was included in every conversation they had and we laughed together often. My least favorite subject in school had become the class that I would find myself looking forward to every day. I felt happier than I had felt in a long time. I finally felt like my life was on the right track. The self-conscious freshman who began high school a year and a half earlier no longer existed and a confident young woman was growing in her place.

As I distanced myself from social life with my old group of friends, an interesting thing began to happen. Other members of the group reached out to tell me that they, too, were unhappy with the way things had progressed within the group. Those who reached out also were struggling to find a new path, and we leaned on each other when we were feeling unsure. The realization that I hadn't been alone in my feelings was liberating and helped to solidify my understanding that I had made the right choice.

While I was becoming closer with my two new friends we were still in the early stages of friendship. Then, one of my old friends from middle school came back into my life. We had met at a summer band camp in fourth grade and again, a year later, when I joined the youth group at my church. We had a rocky relationship during middle school as we were both involved in similar activities and there was a competitive edge to our relationship. However, as we both matured in high school, we reconnected and became close. She became my closest confidante and we spoke constantly. By the end of the summer, the girl who had been my "frenemy" in middle school had become my best friend. She listened to my stories and valued the things I had to say. When I was with her, I felt like I mattered and that through all my hard times there was always someone on my team, rooting for me.

By the end of the summer, it was very clear to me that this was the year I had changed my life. I had learned to stand on my own, and by doing so, had made myself open to new friendships and new opportunities. I learned that, in life, you can't expect others to provide you with your self-worth. You need to claim it and own it and not worry about what anyone thinks. Your happiness is up to you.

As I write this, I am wrapping up my junior year, and it is safe to say that I have never been happier or more confident. I eat lunch with my new friends in the cafeteria every day and we are welcoming to anyone who wishes to join us. Throughout the year, other girls began to sit with us as well and our group expanded. We have a "the more the merrier" mentality and seek to not exclude anyone. My friends continue to fill my life with so much happiness and joy, and I am so grateful to have met each of them, as they were part of a positive change in my life. I don't think that they will ever understand how grateful I am for their friendship and for that one day when they invited me to sit with them in class. That one small act of kindness, which probably didn't hold any significance to them, changed the course of my year, my high school career, and my life.

I am still friendly with the old group of friends. I don't get invited to their parties but it doesn't upset me anymore. I have opened myself up and have made so many new friends who I enjoy spending time with, but I don't rely on them to define who I am. I know who I am, what I enjoy, and what I deserve. I put my time and attention into things I am passionate about, like dance and theater, and I spend no time trying to be popular and fit in.

Needless to say, walking away from my friend group was one of the hardest decisions I have ever made, and I sometimes look back on my life and wonder where I would be if I had stayed in the group. Would I be a different person? I honestly can't answer that question. But without a doubt, I know that I made the right decision. My hope is that the message I've delivered is simply this: be true to yourself. If it doesn't feel right to you, then it's time to walk away. And being different from others doesn't make them or you wrong. But until you value yourself over the acceptance of others, nothing will feel right.

JULIA BOZZA IS A HIGH SCHOOL SENIOR IN NEW JERSEY. SHE LIVES with her two loving parents and three younger brothers in a very noisy house. She wishes to pursue a career in medicine, however, she also loves dancing, musical theatre, and is a member of the mock trial team. This is Julia's first published work and she is very grateful for the opportunity to be able to share her story.

❧ 37 ❧

PHENOMENALITY

BY CATHERINE KREMER

maya angelou once taught me how to be a woman
    phenomenally.
but being a woman in my own body has harbored such a
    complex definition.
i'm a gen z kid, who grew up in the early stages of the internet
        age
impacting my journey of finding self at every turn.
i was taught i was beautiful, my struggle was beautiful,
and it was all totally normal.
true.
i was told i was beautiful without makeup, without pretty
    clothes, without altering my body in any way, even if i
    wanted to.
also true.
but this ideal of beauty created this culture of guilt within
    my mind.
i strove to be this girl that i didn't want to be.
pushed in the direction of not caring about my appearance even
        if i wanted to and turning my nose up at boys even though
        every late night sleepover i would talk about one or more.

it was difficult.
the first time i put on makeup i felt foreign.
caring about clothes felt fake.
my journey became a story of reversing guilt of indulgence
within the things i loved.
a realization that myself, my body, is merely a composition of the
best things i found in other people and the best parts of
my past.
forgetting my appearance, the caked on makeup, the style i strive
to perfect, i have to remember what i truly am.
my tiny body a composition of everything i've ever loved and
ever done.
being a woman in my own body is a complex definition made of
simply nothing less than the most important things in my
life. my heart, my love, and the things i yearn to become.

CATHERINE KREMER, AGE 17, IS A HIGH SCHOOL STUDENT, writer, and spoken word artist. She is a member of the Wordplay Cincy Scribes slam team. She is a Louder Than a Bomb Cincy teen poetry slam finalist. She attended the Denison University Reynolds Young Authors Program and is a winner of numerous Scholastic Keys. She has had work previously published in *FotoFocus, The Poetry of Felix J. Koch*, in partnership with the Cincinnati Museum Center.

❧ 38 ❦

ADVICE FROM MY FUTURE SELF

BY ABBY BYRD

NOTE: TO PROTECT THE IDENTITIES OF MY HIGH SCHOOL FRIENDS, THEIR REAL NAMES HAVE BEEN CHANGED TO THOSE OF WELSH PRINCES.

5-year-old me [knocking on window]: Abby! Abby!

15-year-old me [rising from a restless sleep and stumbling over piles of books, jeans, and flannel shirts to open the window]: Oh my God! Are you me?

35: Yeah. Quick, let me in. I have stuff to tell you about the future.

15 [staring]: Are those wrinkles? [steps back] How much do you weigh?

35: That is a very rude question. Listen, I only have a few minutes. Are you gonna let me in or not?

15 [helping 35 in]: What...How old are you?

35: Thirty-five. And I don't have much time because I was granted only a few minutes between feedings to come see you. So please shut up.

15: Feedings? Do we have a horse?

35: For god's sake, NO! A baby, dipshit!

15: A *BABY*?! At thirty-FIVE?

35: Yes, a baby. Now listen. I need to talk to you about being a woman.

15: Oh, I already got my period.

35: Um... not that. More important things.

15: Hey, I'm married, right? Am I married to William?

35: This is what we need to talk about. The first question you ask your future self shouldn't be if you're married. But since you asked, no. And you need to let go of that obsession. Sorry, but William doesn't like you.

15: [crestfallen] He doesn't?

35: No. I mean, he likes you, but he'll never love you. Don't take it personally, though. He's gay.

15: Gay? You mean like, homosexual? [confused] We have those in our school?

35 [rolls eyes] Christ in a handcart. Yes. Incidentally, everyone except you figured this out during the eighth-grade talent show, when he dry-humped the stage to Madonna's "Express Yourself." And don't count on your backup best friend, either. He's also gay.

15: William *and* Harry are gay? [with rising anxiety]

35: [gently] You know how Harry says everything is "fabulous?" And how he's always late coming to hang out with you because he says he "ran out of gas?"

15: Yeah?

35: Well, "I ran out of gas" is code for "I was engaging in sexual exploration with that guy who lives over on Leeds Avenue."

15 [sits]: This is all very overwhelming. [pauses]

35: Okay, I can see that I'm traumatizing you.

15: [ignoring her] This can't be right. Who will I marry, then?

35: You're doing it again. You're too much of a planner. Stop worrying about the future and just let life happen. You're making things harder for yourself by trying to control everything. Look, I get it. Right now, you think the ultimate fulfillment in life lies in being a wife and mother.

15: I don't think that.

35: You do, Abby. You don't even know you do. You've been conditioned to think that way, to believe that you'll marry right out of college and start a family and life will go trippingly along. That's not going to happen. I can promise you you'll eventually get married, okay? But I won't lie to you. The next two decades of dating and relationships are not going to be pretty. They're going to be like...a sickening carnival ride. It will start out fun, but as you age, the carnival will grow more and more sinister, and each revolution less and less tolerable, until you want to vomit and swear off carnivals forever.

15: [stares]

35: [weakly] Try to think of it as an adventure. You'll travel the country. The world, even! And you'll learn about new things, like Tuvan throat singing and Czech military aircraft. And those are both from the same boyfriend! He also plays the bagpipes! [seeing 15 panic] Uh, scuba diving? Breeding wild cats? Making biodiesel from used cooking oil?

15: [whispering] My God.

35: There are going to be quite a few breakups. After every one, you'll feel afraid and alone. And completely adrift. Once, you'll fall sobbing off your desk chair onto the floor, which will prompt your mother to remark, "Remember, honey, you can't solve your problems with alcohol." But you'll get through it! Not exactly unscathed. I mean, there will be some weird post-traumatic tics. Whenever you see a man playing a mandolin, the murderous rage rising inside you will make it difficult for you to refrain from seizing it and bashing him in the head. And then there's the hissing at passing UPS trucks.

15: I have no idea what you are talking about right now.

35: Okay, never mind. I guess that won't make sense until later. Anyway, your entire twenties are going to pass in a blur of urinary tract infections and bad judgment, and by the time you're 30, you'll be looking at women with engagement rings and measuring yourself against them, wondering what you're doing wrong. You'll even stroll by jewelry stores wistfully and peruse wedding magazines at the pharmacy, the whole time feeling like a fraud. Weddings are seductive. The social approval of being a bride is seductive. But being a princess for a day is different from making a commitment to be someone's partner for life. And neither a wedding nor a marriage is an accomplishment. It's like... you know that floating ducks game at the carnival where you pick up a plastic duck, and if the "magic number" is on that duck, you win a prize?

15: Again with the carnival metaphors.

35: Marriage is like that floating duck game. You don't earn it; it's a matter of luck. You can be the prettiest, wittiest, most charming woman in the world, but whether or not you get married is really just a matter of picking up the right duck.

15: How... how do I pick up the right duck? I mean, how will I know if I pick up the right duck?

35: If you have to ask if it's the right duck, it's probably not the right duck. And I don't want you to consider the relationships that end as wrong ducks mistakes. Every relationship is valuable. But just because you pick up a duck doesn't mean you have to keep it. [pauses] And I will go on record as saying that evaluating potential dates by their facility with the semicolon is a really shitty strategy. As is online dating in general.

15: On...line...dating?

35: In the future, you can... use a computer to talk to people. [glances at Brother® word processor on desk] Forget it; it's too hard to explain. Before I go, I have to tell you about the potatoes.

15: Potatoes.

35: Yeah. Biology complicates the search for a mate. As you get older, the desire to have children can...manipulate your behavior. You might find yourself doing strange things. Like at the grocery store, while holding a five-pound bag of potatoes, you'll bounce them and try to comfort them. It's called "dandling." It's perfectly normal. And just so you know, being pregnant commands even more social approval than getting married. You'll also begin to worry that you won't find a suitable partner to have a baby with. When you find yourself in the same room as a pregnant woman, you'll give a vacuous smile and hollow congratulations, but inside you'll feel...worthless. Dead, like a pile of ashes. Like someone could blow you away. Needless to say, during the parade of pregnancy announcements you'll experience in your late twenties, you're going to have to struggle to muster up some anemic cheers.

15: Rah, rah, reproduction?

35: When it gets overwhelming, I highly recommend taking to your bed with Fudgie the Whale. The cake. To eat, I mean. Not to sleep with.

15: Ew.

35: That feeling you will experience at other women's milestones is fear. You're scared to be alone. You don't know how to be alone. I hate to break this to you, but nothing saves you from being alone, Abby. Nothing. Not marriage, not kids.

15: [tears up] Okay.

35: I gotta go. I love you. Just breathe, all right? There's nothing wrong with you. Oh, and in a few years... can you remember this word for me? Zoloft.

15: Zoloft.

35: [climbing out window] Good girl. [turning back] Oh! And save all that flannel. Hipsters are gonna kill for that vintage in 20 years.

ABBY BYRD's work has appeared on HuffPost and Scary Mommy, *among other sites, and in several anthologies. She runs the blog Little Miss Perfect—a trove of existential angst, biting humor, and bile. Hundreds of clowns once prayed for her en masse; clearly, they achieved nothing. Connect with Abby on Facebook and Goodreads.*

🎇 39 🎇

I'M NOT EVERYBODY'S CUP OF
TEA. AND THAT'S OKAY.

BY JEN MANN

"What's your little book about?" a man asked.

I looked up from the book I was signing. A youngish, clean cut white guy, with no wedding band, and the name "Dave" embroidered on the breast of his neatly pressed polo shirt stood in front of my table. I recognized him immediately. He'd been in the back of the room sort of frowning during my entire speech. I knew the type. This conversation could go one of two ways:

1. He uses dickish behavior as a way to cover up his insecurities, but deep down he really liked what I had to say and needed to hear it, but he needs a few minutes before he can admit it, or

2. He's an asshole.

"Didn't you listen to my talk?" I chided, because I tend to meet hostile remarks with sarcasm.

He grimaced. "You spoke very fast."

I didn't argue. I had a lot to say and not a lot of time to say it.

"Well, my *little* book is actually my third book in a *New York Times* bestselling series of books." I closed the book, revealing the title: *Working with People I Want to Punch in the Throat.*

"Hmm. Sounds violent," he said.

"It's humor, not how-to," I replied, motioning to the next person in line. I ignored Dave so I could speak to the woman who actually wanted to buy a copy of my book.

"Can I at least look at one before I decide if I want it?" Dave asked.

"Of course," I replied. "Help yourself."

He took a copy off the pile and thumbed through it. I ignored his dramatic sighs and tsking (I assumed over my use of f-bombs like commas). My line died down and there were only about six women left when Dave barged up to the table again, ignoring the women he'd cut in line. He held up the book. "This list," he said, shaking the book at me. "What is this?"

"It's my Punch List," I said. "I make a list for all my books. They give you an idea of the topics I'm going to cover in the essays."

He read aloud, "Mansplainers." He grunted and rolled his eyes.

Oh, great. He's an asshole with absolutely no sense of humor, I thought.

"I don't think you even know what mansplaining is," Dave snapped.

The women gaped at Dave.

I smiled coolly. "The fact that you're telling me that I don't know what the word means is incredible," I said. "I don't think *you* know what it means."

The women giggled.

That was all it took. What is that quote from Margaret Atwood? *"Men are afraid women will laugh at them, women are afraid men will kill them."* I felt like that. I saw the shift in Dave. I watched his eyes go dark and his face go hard. If we'd been sort of ribbing one another before, now it was on like Donkey Kong. Dave wanted to go to war.

Dave glowered. "Oh yeah, well, what do you call a woman who thinks she knows it all?"

The women gasped softly.

"I'm smart, so I'd call her *right*," I said, looking straight into his eyes, refusing to look away or cower.

The women chuckled.

Dave fumed and glared at me. "You're not everybody's cup of tea," he spat, his mouth curled into a mean-spirited sneer.

The women exclaimed and Dave looked triumphant.

Here's the thing, Dave had been trying to get a rise out of me and up until that point, I'd refused to take the bait. But I knew men like Dave. I've dealt with many Dave's over the years. You see, I write a lot of observations on everything from politics to pop culture to parenting. My opinions can be a bit polarizing at times and although the bulk of people who read my work like what I have to say, there is always someone who disagrees. No matter what I write, I tend to receive harsh criticism and backlash on just about any topic. I am known as someone who likes to "stir the pot" and sometimes when I'm at an event like that one, I get someone who decides they'll try and stir my pot. Dave had brought his own spoon.

I considered Dave's words. They were meant to hurt me. They were a jab at me. He was telling me what so many men (and even a few women) had been telling me over the years:

"Pipe down over there!"

"Shut your yap!"

"Do what you do best: make us laugh!"

"No one cares what you think! You are nobody!"

Anytime I've crossed a line where I offended or insulted or even simply irked a man with my opinion, he has been quick to lash out at me. To tell me that I'm just some fat housewife in Middle America who doesn't know shit. I've been called every name in the book, I've been threatened with violence, my family has been threatened, and yet I continue to raise my voice.

"Why?" you ask.

Because many years ago I found my voice and I found my tribe. I found that I could say the things that others couldn't. I could speak for the ones who were unable to speak up or who weren't brave enough. I could speak for the ones who felt like their ideas were meaningless. I could speak for the ones who felt alone and unseen. The one's who apologized for merely existing. I'm not everybody's cup of tea, but I'm *their* cup of tea and that was the part Dave couldn't understand.

I still hadn't responded, so Dave tried again. "What do you have to say to your haters?"

I laughed loudly. (Because so many men like Dave hate that. They hate how much space I take up, how much air I use, how loud I am.) "I say, who cares about them?" I snarled.

Dave was incredulous. "What? You don't care what people think of you?" he demanded.

"That's exactly right, Dave," I replied, taking the wind completely out of his sails.

"But, but," he sputtered. "I can't believe it, but you actually sound like you're okay with that!"

"Here's the thing, Dave. There are only four people in this world whose opinions I care about: my husband, my two kids, and my own. Everyone else can get lost. You are not the first person to ask me this question and you won't be the last, but I am done trying to be everybody's cup of tea. I reach the people who need me and those are the people I write for. I don't care if you hate what I have to say. I don't care if it bruises your ego or hurts your feelings or makes you think or whatever set you off. I have no plans to change who I am and if you don't like what I have to say, I suggest you move on and find someone else to talk to, because you are blocking my table and the people who actually want to speak to me."

I snatched my book out of Dave's hands and his mouth flapped open and closed, but no sound came out. I stared him down, unwavering. Inside I wavered a bit, because while I knew I was right and I was not afraid to poke the bear, one of these days I will get punched in the face by some pissed off dude and I still had another appearance that night and I didn't want a black eye—although it would have looked badass and I'd have a great story to tell, but still.

Dave lurked around my table for the rest of the event. He challenged anyone who approached me. "What do think of this stuff she writes?" he'd demand. Almost everyone ignored him or brushed him off, including me. I never spoke to Dave again and I refused to acknowledge his presence. I would not give that troll any sunlight in which to grow.

When I got back to the hotel that night I called my family and told them to story. My daughter was on the phone. "You have haters?" she asked, sadly.

I shrugged. "Yeah, so?"

"And you don't care?" Her nine-year-old brain couldn't comprehend. In those days she was dealing with her own mean-girl antics at school and she was working overtime to convince those girls to be her friend. She couldn't understand the idea of completely writing off people instead.

"Why should I care what someone thinks of me?" I replied. "That's on them. They are the ones who spend their time worrying about what I'm up to and what I'm doing. They're the ones taking time out of their busy lives to let me know just how much they think I suck. Dave spent an hour today of his life trying to make me feel bad. He's the one who wasted his time. I got work done, I made money, and I met new people. Dave is the loser here," I said.

"But don't you want everyone to like you?" she asked. "If they don't like you, they won't buy your books. That guy didn't buy a book, did he?"

I shook my head. "I don't do this to sell books. Selling books is a nice thing, but that's not why I write what I write. I write because I need to and my audience needs me to. We need each other. They are my people."

"Doesn't it hurt your feelings to know people don't like you?" my daughter said, her voice thick with emotion. I imagined the tears brimming in her eyes.

"It's taken me a long time to get to this point," I said. "That's why I need you to learn faster than me."

"Learn what?"

"No one can make us feel bad about ourselves unless we let them make us feel bad. Yes, my love, I am not everybody's cup of tea. Dave was right about that. But, do not worry about the people who don't like your tea. Find your tea-drinkers. Those are your people."

This is something that took me 25 years to master. Twenty-five very long years. I wish my mother had told me this in kindergarten when I came home in tears because an older girl (probably a first grader, but she seemed very worldly to me in those days) made fun of my awesome striped knee socks and I refused to ever wear them again. I wish my mother had told me this in sixth grade when I developed faster than other girls and the boys were relentless with their teasing and their constant attempts to grope me. I wish my mother had told me this in tenth grade when I moved from New Jersey to Kansas and I had to figure out how to fit my East Coast cynicism and sarcasm in with the pearl-clutching Midwestern kids. It was a hard lesson to learn, but I finally did. I don't care what others think of me. I don't try to keep up with my neighbors anymore or compare myself to my friends. I don't stress over fitting into the right wardrobe or having a magazine-worthy home. I don't allow myself to suffer from mommy guilt or second-guess my parenting. In the, now immortal, words of Elsa, *I let it go*. And I've never been happier.

Once my daughter was born, I vowed I would always try to teach this lesson to her. To show her that you never need to change who you are, rather you need to find the people who like you for you. Embrace your quirks, know your strengths, celebrate your differences, find your happiness inside, rather than seeking it elsewhere. Laugh at yourself, rage against injustice, be loud, be soft, be tough, be girly, get dirty, cry, dream, imagine, work hard, have it all. You do you, my love.

JEN MANN IS BEST KNOWN FOR HER WILDLY POPULAR AND HYSTERICAL blog People I Want to Punch in the Throat. She has been described by many as Erma Bombeck—with f-bombs. Jen is known for her hilarious rants and funny observations. Jen is the author of the New York Times *bestseller* People I Want to Punch in the Throat: Competitive Crafters, Drop-Off Despots, and Other Suburban Scourges *which was a Finalist for a Goodreads Reader's Choice Award. Her latest book is* My Lame Life: Queen of the Misfits, *her first fiction book for young adults. She is also the master-mind behind the* New York Times *bestselling* I Just Want to Pee Alone *series.*

NOTES FROM THE EDITOR

Thank you for reading this collection of essays. I appreciate your support and I hope you enjoyed it. I also hope you will tell a friend—or 30 about this. Please do me a huge favor and leave me a review. Of course I prefer 5-star, but I'll take what I can get. If you hated this book, you can skip the review. *Namaste.*

OTHER BOOKS AVAILABLE

People I Want to Punch in the Throat: Competitive Crafters, Drop Off Despots, and Other Suburban Scourges

Spending the Holidays with People I Want to Punch in the Throat: Yuletide Yahoos, Ho-Ho-Humblebraggers, and Other Seasonal Scourges

Working with People I Want to Punch in the Throat: Cantankerous Clients, Micromanaging Minions, and Other Supercilious Scourges

My Lame Life: Queen of the Misfits

OTHER ANTHOLOGIES AVAILABLE

I Just Want to Pee Alone

I STILL Just Want to Pee Alone

I Just Want to Be Alone

I Just Want to Be Perfect

But Did You Die?

OTHER SINGLES AVAILABLE

Just a Few People I Want to Punch in the Throat (Vol. 1)
   Just a Few People I Want to Punch in the Throat (Vol. 2)
   Just a Few People I Want to Punch in the Throat (Vol. 3)
   Just a Few People I Want to Punch in the Throat (Vol. 4)
   Just a Few People I Want to Punch in the Throat (Vol. 5)
   Just a Few People I Want to Punch in the Throat (Vol. 6)

Made in the USA
Lexington, KY
29 September 2018